Goodbye
Shahzadi

Goodbye Shahzadi

A POLITICAL BIOGRAPHY OF BENAZIR BHUTTO

SHYAM BHATIA

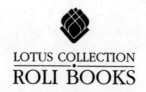

LOTUS COLLECTION
ROLI BOOKS

≈

For the women who changed my life:
my wife, Amanda
and
my mother, Shakuntala

≈

Lotus Collection

This edition in 2008
The Lotus Collection
An imprint of
Roli Books Pvt. Ltd
M-75, G.K. II Market, New Delhi 110 048
Phones: ++91 (011) 2921 2271, 2921 2782
2921 0886, Fax: ++91 (011) 2921 7185
E-mail: roli@vsnl.com
Website: rolibooks.com
Also at
Varanasi, Bangalore, Kolkata, Jaipur & Mumbai

Cover design: Supriya Saran
Layout design: Narendra Shahi

ISBN: 978-81-7436-658-0

Typeset in Centaur MT by Roli Books Pvt. Ltd and
printed at Rekmo, New Delhi.

CONTENTS

ACKNOWLEDGEMENTS   vii

AUTHOR'S NOTE   ix

1 The Shahzadi Arrives   I

2 Her Father's Daughter   11

3 The Marriage Business   28

4 A Startling Revelation   38

5 The American Connection   44

6 The India Link   58

7 The Nuclear Game   67

8 Dealing with the Generals   80

9 The Years in Power   89

10 Exile   104

EPILOGUE   114

INDEX   127

CONTENTS

ACKNOWLEDGEMENTS

FRIENDS AND CONTACTS ACROSS THREE CONTINENTS GAVE THEIR UNSTINTING HELP IN THE PREPARATION OF this book. In Delhi it was Kuldip Nayar who first encouraged me to write a biography of Benazir incorporating material from some of my past interviews. In London my older son, Rupert, pushed me to use his laptop exclusively for the book. My younger son, Crispin, helped unfathom the mysteries of the Internet. My friend and neighbour, Saleem Naqvi, read one of the earlier drafts. David Watts, my friend and colleague of many years standing, read the whole manuscript in one sitting and suggested amendments. So too did Professor Steve Alpern. Philip Knightley generously gave up some of his time to read and comment on the book. Wajid Shamsul Hasan patiently answered endless questions. John Fisher Burns, a former *New York Times* bureau chief in Delhi, kindly agreed to share some of his Pakistan experiences. In Washington, Peter Galbraith helped fill some of the gaps in the years leading up to and beyond Benazir's first term in office. So too did Mark Siegel. Selig Harrison, a South Asia expert of great distinction agreed to give his overview of the finished product. Pramod Kapoor, publisher of Roli Books, was a wise and principled guide from start to finish. Nandita Bhardwaj and Adil Tyabji were model editors. To each of them, and to those others who prefer to remain anonymous, I send my heartfelt thanks.

ACKNOWLEDGMENTS

AUTHOR'S NOTE

I INTERVIEWED BENAZIR BHUTTO ON INNUMERABLE OCCASIONS, MORE OFTEN INDEED THAN ANY OTHER politician I have ever known. The reason was simple. We met in Oxford and remained in touch thereafter.

Until I met Benazir, Pakistan for me conjured images of mad mullahs, forced conversions and oppressed women backed up by a theology of hate that refused to accept anyone belonging to a different value system. Benazir was poles removed from this mental picture. She did not speak of religion unless specifically asked, did not wear a veil, was certainly not oppressed, and, above all, was prepared to engage in open debate among equals, male or female, on any conceivable issue.

Cynics might argue that my distaste for jihadi culture meant that I was far too accepting of someone like Benazir, gratefully seizing upon her apparently liberal outlook at face value and overlooking any flaws of character, such as an inbuilt opportunism. In retrospect, such a judgement seems less than fair. Like so many of us at the time, Benazir was more a free-thinking student than a two-faced politician. Insofar as she had any plans for the future, they had to do with her desire to join her country's diplomatic service.

When we got to know each other better, she would theorize that the

Bhuttos, Bhatias, and Bhattis were all part of the same Rajput family tree that had its roots in southern Afghanistan. Over the centuries, branches of this vast extended family moved eastwards, she believed, modifying their clan name and their religious persuasion in keeping with the local circumstances in which they found themselves. If that was true, our common Rajput ancestry gave us something in common, as did the time we spent at Oxford. Our family circumstances were however very different. My father was a journalist who strayed into the Indian Foreign Service and back again into journalism. His journalism gave him access to all manner of people from all walks of life, including Benazir's father Zulfikar Ali Bhutto.

I still recall the story my father related of meeting and interviewing Zulfikar for the *Indian Express* in the early 1960s. The interview was in Calcutta and my father was accompanied by the *Indian Express* cartoonist who proceeded to hastily sketch Zulfikar, then the foreign minister of Pakistan. Asked by the nervous cartoonist if he would autograph his work, Zulfikar, who was balding, looked at the cartoon and commented, 'I've got more hair around my private parts than he's given me at the top of my head.'

The Bhuttos were wealthy feudal landlords from Sindh, not dissimilar to old fashioned English squires who lived off the land and the rents of their tenants. Zulfikar, later tried and executed for a murder he protested he never ordered, was the first casualty in a dynasty of death that would go on, before their time, to claim the lives of his older daughter and two sons. When Zulfikar died, his widow and children inherited at least 12,000 acres of land in Larkana, about an hour's flying time from Karachi.

What set Benazir apart from many of her Pakistani contemporaries was a self-evidently progressive outlook that found expression in a book she wrote only months before she was assassinated. 'The vast majority of the billion Muslims in the world embrace a peaceful, tolerant, open, rational, and loving religion,' wrote Benazir. 'This is the interpretation of Islam that my father ... and mother ... taught my brothers ... my sister ... and me.' Some of Benazir's critics have questioned the sincerity of these apparently liberal convictions; in her own defence she argued that she had changed and matured with the passage of time.

Flitting between Oxford and London, where the Pakistani High Commissioner had invited her to treat his residence as a second home, she was extremely glamorous and brought a zing of excitement to our day-to-day lives as university students. It did not seem obvious at the time, but now, looking back, Benazir seemed to be almost bubble-wrapped in a kind of all-encompassing innocence and that added to her appeal.

Our last contact was in October 2007, just before she went back home after a decade of exile to take part in national elections planned for early 2008. The setting was a crowded press conference in London where we just managed to exchange a few words. She was looking much older than I remembered, and jowly. There was no sparkle to her voice, or her face. Why are you going back, I asked in bewilderment? She muttered something about it being too late to back out. How about an interview? I continued. Send me the questions, she replied, and I will get back to you. I didn't follow up my request, but to my surprise a few weeks later I had a phone call from Pakistan with a familiar voice asking, 'So where are the questions?' I had no alternative but to respond, and the result was one of the last interviews she gave before she was shot dead in front of her adoring supporters.

Some of the students who were at Oxford in 1972–75, including Indians and Pakistanis, stood out because they were from famous families, although a few but not all them would go on to make a name for themselves in their own right. They included a young English aristocrat at Christ Church, Benazir's brother's college, who had neither the intellect nor the application to be admitted to such a world-renowned university. Rumour had it that he was accepted because his father had promised to gift 800 years of private family papers to the college or university libraries, in exchange for his son's guaranteed admission.

Then there were the Americans, usually supported by extremely generous grants, who always seemed to come across as the most gifted and hard-working members of the student body. They included Peter Galbraith, son of the American economist and former US ambassador to India, John Kenneth Galbraith, who had been friendly with Benazir during her earlier Harvard years. He would play a vital role in later years in freeing her from the clutches of the Pakistani military.

Among those from South Asia, many, whether they knew it or not at the time, were destined for greater things. Imran Khan became a world-class cricketer, Vikram Seth, who would bob up unexpectedly on the narrow winding streets that linked the colleges of Oxford, would develop into a writer of international renown. Benazir was different. She arrived as a ready-made celebrity because she was the daughter of Prime Minister Zulfikar Ali Bhutto, the leader of an important country that was in the process of rebuilding itself after the 1971 war with India and the loss of its eastern wing that emerged as the independent state of Bangladesh.

The war had led to the loss of thousands of innocent lives, and millions of refugees. When we first met, Indian and Pakistani, reading for our respective degrees on the same English university campus, Benazir and I were soon at daggers drawn. We could not agree whether or not her father was responsible for the war and whether, in the wake of such a disastrous conflict, he should be awarded an honorary degree at Oxford.

To her abiding credit, Benazir did not allow our subsequent dealings to be permanently affected by my negative views about her father; for my part, I sent a letter of condolence to her in Pakistan after Zulfikar was executed and then made the effort to call on her in London. I also took the time to call on her in London after her younger brother, Shahnawaz, was killed by poisoning in Cannes. After she was toppled from office in 1996 we met more regularly, sometimes two or three times a year, in London or Dubai. She always inquired after my wife, whom she had met, and our two children who were in the same age bracket as her own. Our conversations occasionally degenerated into farce because of her fondness for mimicking the political leaders she and I knew in common. Benazir was also curious about war reporting and

GOODBYE SHAHZADI

XII

my life experiences as a Cairo- and Jerusalem-based journalist, repeatedly asking what it was like to live among the Jews in Israel. In 1995 she sent a message to me in Jerusalem to say that she was thinking of visiting Gaza and inquiring whether I would be around. That visit never materialized, but Benazir ensured that she was always up to date about the historic Middle East conflict dividing Jews and Arabs.

In 2003 and 2004 she agreed to a series of searingly honest interviews on the record with me about herself, her family, and her political life. At the time I did publish some, but not all the material from the tapes of those interviews. Some tapes containing much of the unpublished material, including her revelations about Pakistan's nuclear programme, remained locked away in my filing cabinet. They only came to light by chance soon after she was assassinated when I was scouring through my personal papers in search of some other documents. I realized then that the tapes contained exclusive information about contemporary issues that had never before been revealed.

I also got to know her brother Murtaza at Oxford. A year younger than Benazir, he and I shared the same academic supervisor in our postgraduate research about the history of the nuclear programmes of India and Pakistan. Some years later, when I encountered Murtaza in exile in Damascus, he told me with some bitterness that it was he who had been designated as the political heir of their father Zulfikar. As evidence, Murtaza told me how it was he and not Benazir who had been asked to manage their father's Larkana constituency during the 1977 General Election. This was a conviction shared by at least one senior member of Zulfikar's staff, Yusuf Buch, who told his friend and fellow staffer Khalid Hasan that the prime minister would rather his daughter was spared the rough and tumble of politics, preferring that she join Pakistan's Foreign Service.

It was a point of view vigorously disputed by Benazir during her lifetime, claiming that her father had always wanted her to enter politics. She was, however, wrong on one count when she cited as evidence her father's decision to deliberately include her in the delegation that went to the famous India–Pakistan summit in S[h]imla in 1972. There was nothing deliberate about that decision. Zulfikar had originally intended to take his wife Nusrat to that summit, but she fell ill and Benazir was a hurried, last minute choice to fill in for her mother. Now that Benazir and Murtaza are both dead, the baton has been passed on to their respective sets of children. Pakistan's future could well be affected by how this next generation of Bhuttos manage their competing interests. Benazir, Murtaza, Shahnawaz, and their father cannot expect to rest easy in the family graveyard in Larkana.

I

THE SHAHZADI ARRIVES

SHAHZADI (PRINCESS), PINKIE (THE PET NAME GIVEN TO HER BY HER PARENTS), PRIME MINISTER, MOHTARMA (respected lady), BB, 'Miss Sahiba', and 'Yank' were among the names—some of them used tongue-in-cheek—by which I addressed Benazir Bhutto during our 34-year association. We were not always the best of friends, but we were in regular contact for much of the time and, occasionally, I was entrusted with confidential insights.

The range of names were a pointer to the different things she had done in her life, to that extent depicting her multi-faceted personality, but they also hinted at some fundamental contradictions. The 'Yank' who arrived at Oxford with an American accent from Harvard also happened to be a Pakistani who in later years could 'wow' the crowds back home with Sindhi-language taunts of Pakistan's many military dictators. She revelled in her aristocratic feudal background, but liked those close to her to call her BB or even Pinkie. After she became prime minister in 1989, party workers were encouraged to refer to her as Mohtarma.

If these puzzlingly different titles sowed confusion in the minds of outsiders, so did her lifestyle. In Pakistan she was to all intents and purposes a deeply conservative Muslim woman who covered her head in public and sought to uphold the many rules and social traditions handed down to the Islamic community many hundreds of years ago by Prophet Mohammed.

Back in Oxford, however, she followed a lifestyle that would have seemed repugnant to traditionalists in her own and other Muslim countries. It was not just the yellow MG sports car gifted to her by her father—on which I and others would sometimes leave messages—that gave her a personal freedom denied to most women in Pakistan (in the fellow Islamic state of Saudi Arabia, for example, women are forbidden by law to drive). There were however also the casual jeans and T-shirts she liked to wear, the occasional glass of white wine she liked to drink, and a myriad of mostly white boyfriends with whom she socialized that would have raised eyebrows in the deepest reaches of Sindh, where she was born, and the Punjabi heartlands of Pakistan.

At Oxford, and later back home in Pakistan, Benazir declared herself an ardent supporter of women's rights. Given her gender that was only to be expected. She certainly appointed women to senior government jobs, but then, in order to win the support of Islamic radicals, she agreed to sustain draconian Pakistani legislation that underlies the inferior status of women. This was especially true when it came to legislation involving rape, where the burden of proof remained on women.

As Asma Jehangir of the Pakistan Human Rights Commission would comment during Benazir's second term in office, 'The fact remains that Benazir does not have the courage or sometimes the support to do away with laws that actually encourage men to commit crimes against women.' Another human rights activist commented sardonically, 'In a Muslim society [like Pakistan], if Asif Ali Zardari, her husband, were to turn Benazir out of the house, she would be entitled to only Rs 32.50 [less than one US dollar] compensation.'

At Oxford, Benazir participated in rational, scientific discourse that culminated in her gaining a degree in politics, philosophy, and economics (PPE) at Lady Margaret Hall. Back home, she revealed herself as no different from the village women of her home province who swear by faith healers and other superstitious practices.

She was serving as prime minister for the second time in 1994 when she made a lengthy journey to distant Bangladesh purely to seek the benediction of a local holy man in her fight against political enemies. The 'holy man' gave her a charm and a magic word that she was told to repeat 250,000 times to guarantee her political and physical survival.

For all her commitment to democratic ideals and improving the lot of the common man and woman, Benazir at university epitomized the classic spoilt rich girl from a third world country. She was self-obsessed, liked to have her own way, and her temper tantrums were legendary. One particular story about the Bhutto homestead in Larkana became the talking point for months in Oxford's junior and middle common rooms.

It was the autumn of 1974 and I was at a party where one particular woman student, a college friend of Benazir's from Lady Margaret Hall, was holding forth about how she had spent part of the previous summer at the Bhutto family home, Al Murtaza, in Larkana. Asked if she had enjoyed the visit, the student friend replied, 'I'm never going back there. When Pinkie loses her temper [which she apparently often did], she throws ashtrays like flying saucers at the servants.'

The tantrums notwithstanding, she was an attractive, some would say compelling, personality. Her deep throaty laugh was recognizable at a 100 paces and she was generous to a fault, always paying her way in restaurants and sometimes picking up the tab for everyone who was at her table. She could also be extremely funny, occasionally mimicking the body language of people she knew.

Although respectful of Indira Gandhi in every way, one of Benazir's set pieces on campus was to re-tell in every detail how the two of them met at the 1972 S[h]imla summit and how Mrs Gandhi's gimlet eyes seemingly followed her into every nook and cranny. 'I don't think she liked all that free and favourable publicity I was getting in the Indian Press,' Benazir commented. Her own brand of humour remained with her long after she left Oxford, and it was underwritten by her own special language for those like General Zia ul Haq who had harmed her family. In my presence she always added a touch of spice when talking about Zia, sometimes calling him 'Zia ul Muck' or 'Cobra Eyes'.

For us South Asians at Oxford it was not just Benazir's obvious star qualities that drew us to her. She had a human side that was just as attractive. When an immigration official was rude to her at London's Heathrow airport, her re-telling of the incident found an echo in each of our hearts. The official had asked how she planned to fund her stay at Oxford. When she explained she was supported by her parents, the official behind the desk sneered, 'How can a Paki have enough money for an Oxford education?'

An educated, modern woman who became an icon for women's rights all over the world, Benazir nevertheless consented to an arranged marriage with a man who was her intellectual and social inferior, and who went on to father their three children. It was a complete travesty for her to claim years later that her public persona did not allow her to lead the sort of life that would permit the cultivation of a relationship evolving into marriage.

In those Oxford years she was madly in love with two extremely handsome Pakistani students. Although marital inquiries made on her behalf were firmly rebuffed in both cases, Benazir continued to pursue her interest in one of them, later even offering him a job as a government adviser as part of a lifetime package. Asif Zardari, the man she eventually agreed to marry, was the son of a provincial cinema owner and came a very poor third in the scale of her lifetime's needs and desires.

The wonder of wonders was that she was even prepared to socially interact with students from India, Pakistan's historic enemy, without allowing their conversations to degenerate into sessions of recrimination and mutual abuse. Karan Thapar, who went on to become a famous television presenter, was one of them. Neena Gopal, a reporter, and later foreign editor of *Gulf News*, became a regular companion during her years of exile in Dubai.

How did Benazir herself reconcile to these contradictions? The key or connecting link was her desire to be liked, to be popular, and for that she was prepared to be all things to all people. This would become a recurrent theme in her later years too, explaining why she could be equally at ease with Marxists and capitalists, Indians and Israelis, Islamic fundamentalists and liberal democrats, Chinese, Australians, in fact anyone on the planet.

The chameleon-like quality that enabled her to blend into any and every background made her irresistible to the Western media in particular. After she was assassinated, one British newspaper reporter recalled a memorable lunch with Benazir at the RAF Club in London. Another remembered an email response, with Benazir declaring, 'Thanks a million for writing to me ... Hpe u come back and we visit here again.' Part of this easy familiarity was facilitated by her thorough grasp of the English language; it is difficult to imagine a woman politician from, say Libya or Togo, matching her language fluency and blending it with her natural charm to advance the cause she represented.

Some of Benazir's more memorable media encounters were with breathless 'celebrity interviewers' like Daphne Barak, who doubles as an American–Israeli television producer in the US and described her Pakistani friend as a 'girlie-girl who loved to talk about skin care and hair styles'. It was Barak who revealed Benazir's passion for Italian and French food, and how she cared about what she looked like under clothes. It was also Barak who introduced her to Victoria's Secret lingerie and Pria face and body cream. When Benazir was under house arrest in November 2007, Barak telephoned to ask if she could send her face cream or perfume. Benazir replied that she had a more urgent need for a bulldozer.

Another celebrity contact, this one from London, also described Benazir as a 'close friend', and related how they went shopping for groceries one night when Benazir bought tinned tomatoes and volunteered her special recipe for Baked Alaska 'using meringues, fruit and piles of ice cream'.

I found her captivating, charismatic, and intriguing from the time we first met in 1973. She had just completed an undergraduate degree at Harvard's Radcliffe College and was now preparing for a second undergraduate degree in PPE. There was no particular reason for our paths to cross. Oxford had a student body of some 12,000, including my own men's only institution, Wadham, and they were spread out across the city. The fact that I was pursuing postgraduate research also made it even less likely that we would run across each other at lectures or seminars. As an undergraduate, she would attend lectures for, say 50 or 60 students. As a postgraduate preparing for a PhD, I would have one-to-one sessions with my supervisor. Undergraduates socialized in junior common rooms; postgraduates had middle common rooms.

What initially brought us together was my freelance work for BBC Radio in London. One of the producers there casually suggested that an interview with Benazir might be a good idea, and I was duly dispatched to knock on her door. Benazir opened the door dressed in her pyjamas and dressing gown. She had no make-up on her face and a vertical scar, either a birthmark or of an injury, was clearly visible on one side of her face.

I did not know it at the time, but this was the first of a series of interviews that would stretch over three decades before and after she became prime minister of Pakistan. Some of the interviews were more formal than others, some more revealing about policy issues. When she was at her lowest ebb after being removed from office in 1993, I was given some astounding insights into Pakistan's nuclear and missile programmes. Benazir however never forgot that first encounter.

She was skittish about the first interview in Oxford, saying she would have to first clear it with her father, but was perfectly willing to engage in off-the-record social chit-chat over a cup of coffee. Our shared South Asian heritage gave us a lot to talk about, with Benazir repeatedly asking for my views on Indira Gandhi whom she had met only a year earlier. As I left, I told her, 'Well, I guess it's *salaam aleikum* until we meet again.' Benazir looked at me wide-eyed. 'How come you are saying *salaam aleikum*, you're not a Muslim.' We parted on friendly terms, but our subsequent encounters as young idealistic students did not always run smoothly. It was the 'I' word for India and the 'P' word for Pakistan about which we each held strong views and did not always see eye-to-eye.

One specific issue about which we disagreed was over her passionate desire to persuade Oxford to award her father, Zulfikar, an honorary degree. The elder Bhutto had been at Oxford some twenty years earlier and had loved it. It was at his insistence that Benazir first, and then Murtaza, applied for admission to their respective colleges.

Bhutto's tutor back in 1950 was a rising academic star, Hugh Trevor Roper, who in our time became the Regius professor of history. He was an influential man on the faculty and at the university in general, and it was with his support that Benazir spearheaded the campaign for her father's honorary degree. I led the student opposition, disgusted by what we saw as Zulfikar's ignoble role in persecuting Sheikh Mujibur Rahman and his followers who, supported by India in 1971, eventually broke away from Pakistan and created their own independent state of Bangladesh.

Terrible stories about Pakistani army atrocities filled the media throughout 1970 and 1971, and there was a question mark over the political role Zulfikar had played. At the time Benazir was at Harvard, and for a brief period in 1971 her father press-ganged her into helping him present Pakistan's case at the UN Security Council in New York. One of her tasks was to act as a mascot, telephone reporter, and receptionist for her father in his hotel suite where he received an endless stream of delegations from concerned governments. 'Interrupt the meetings,' Zulfikar told his daughter. 'If the Soviets are here, tell me the Chinese are calling. If the Americans are here, tell me the Russians are on the line, or the Indians. And don't tell anyone who is actually here.'

For all his fancy diplomatic footwork, Pakistan was forced to surrender and relinquish its Eastern half. India won the 1971 war and Bangladesh came into existence but the stories about Pakistani war atrocities and what Zulfikar could have done to prevent them never really went away. They continued to resonate in Oxford where Benazir failed abysmally to persuade the university to award her father the much sought after honorary degree. For several weeks Benazir and I stopped speaking to each other; sometimes there were shouting matches outside our respective colleges.

Many years later Benazir admitted her own woeful ignorance of what had been going on in East Pakistan which she ruefully conceded had been treated as a colony by her fellow countrymen from the Western part of the country. 'How many times have I asked God to forgive me for my ignorance?' Benazir wrote several years later. Back in 1973, however, there was little evidence of such humility.

Indeed, after our verbal spats over the issue of the honorary degree there was tangible hostility between us for over six months, which ended when I received an invitation to a drinks party jointly hosted by Benazir and Peter Galbraith, a fellow student, to launch her career in student politics.

'So you have stopped speaking to me?' Benazir inquired as I arrived at the party. 'Pinkie,' I replied in Urdu, 'who am I to ignore a *shahzadi*?' I was not sure whether she sensed my sarcasm or simply chose to ignore it. It did not matter because from then onwards we remained on friendly terms. At Oxford I also got to know Benazir's brother, Mir Murtaza, who like his sister had earlier been at Harvard. The two were in age only a year apart and Murtaza followed his sister to Oxford in 1974. In those days brother and sister were on friendly teasing terms with each other, although the fact that Murtaza's college was at the other end of the city did not encourage closeness. Murtaza was far less outgoing than his sister, and we only got to know each other because we shared the same tutor, Sir Michael Howard, and there were some occasions when we met outside Sir Michael's rooms at All Souls.

After Benazir was forced out of office for the second time we met at least once or twice a year, sometimes for a cup of tea in the afternoon and at other times for lunch. On these occasions she would always greet me with the same teasing remark, 'Shyam, I am not going to be interviewed by you because I always tell you more than I should,' and, as ever, she did. These get-togethers were usually occasions to chew the cud over the latest developments in Pakistan and Islamabad's relations with the outside world. She was always keen to understand the bigger picture, which was probably why she liked to talk to me, an Indian, to discuss these things and gauge how I viewed them.

The most indiscreet she permitted herself to be was in Dubai in 2003 where I had stopped on my way back to London from Delhi. Just before leaving Delhi, Benazir had emailed me her Dubai address, inviting me to spend the day and stay for dinner with her family. Benazir's three children sat quietly in the far corner of the room before we sat down for the meal, Nusrat was upstairs being attended to by nurses. After dinner, when the children were upstairs in bed, we talked and talked for hours. We laughed about our Oxford days, Benazir told me how much she had loved her father and her love for Pakistan. There were tears too, with a weeping Benazir telling me at one point in graphic and horrifying detail of her father's shameful treatment in prison and how he had been starved and tormented by the authorities in the hope that he would collapse and die in his cell.

Her most extraordinary revelation was about her personal role in exporting Pakistan's precious nuclear secrets to North Korea in exchange for Pyongyang's missile technology. She made me turn off my tape-recorder as she gleefully related the details. A year later in London when I asked her to repeat the Korean story on tape, she refused to do so, side-stepping the issue and moving on to something else.

Another nugget picked up over dinner amidst much laughter was her memory as a 19-year-old of attending the 1972 India–Pakistan S[h]imla summit with her father. Benazir's presence at that summit sent out a message that she had ambitions of her own. That ambition in those days may only have extended to becoming one of Pakistan's future ambassadors, but whatever it was, the very strength of her personality suggested a major future role for Benazir Bhutto. No wonder then that after executing her father, Pakistan's military dictator, General Zia ul Haq, placed her under house arrest before packing her off into exile.

I interviewed General Zia several times for the *Observer* of London.

At all the interviews I routinely asked him when he was going to let Benazir return to Pakistan. At our last interview Zia said, 'Mr Bhatia, your wish has finally been granted; Benazir is being allowed to return home.' When I asked him why, he replied with a sigh, 'Democracy is a bitter pill which we must swallow.'

Someone must have repeated this conversation to Benazir as evidence of my loyalty to her. When she did fly back to Lahore in 1987, she arranged for me to ride with her in the lead lorry that took us to Iqbal Park at Minar-e-Pakistan, where she addressed an about two million-strong crowd.

Months later, Zia was killed in a plane crash, and following the elections Benazir became prime minister. During that time we had no contact, yet I remember as if it was yesterday Benazir telling me with such sorrow that she was convinced that General Zia had personally ordered the murder of her younger brother, Shahnawaz, and that elements of the Pakistan military were behind Murtaza's death.

As for herself, Benazir said in one of her memorable interviews with me, her grassroots popularity had been a thorn in Zia's side and of his successors. 'Therefore, for a series of people I must be eliminated. The first successor [Zia] tried to eliminate me to impose a one-party rule in the country. Now the military again wants to eliminate me because they want the MMA, the alliance of religious parties, to be the only alternative in the country.'

2

HER FATHER'S DAUGHTER

ZULFIKAR ALI BHUTTO DEFINED HIS DAUGHTER'S FUTURE IN A WAY THAT NEITHER HE, NOR NUSRAT, HIS WIFE OF Iranian origin, nor Benazir herself could have anticipated. By taking Benazir on foreign trips, including those to the United Nations in New York, and by introducing her to famous foreign dignitaries, he encouraged her to take an interest in his world of international politics. During her formative years he was at the epicentre of Pakistani politics and she, at an impressionable age, witnessed his many highs and lows. When he was hanged, both his sons were in exile and it was left to Benazir in Pakistan, supported by her mother, to defend his memory and carry the burden of his legacy as best she could.

Zulfikar was a lawyer by profession. He attended secondary school in Bombay before being accepted at the University of Southern California, from where he graduated with a degree in political science. In 1943, when he was 15, Zulfikar's marriage was arranged according to local custom with a fellow Sindhi, Shireen Amir Begum, who outlived him by 24 years. In practice the couple spent no time together. Zulfikar was 19 when he enrolled at the University of Southern California. From there he moved on to Oxford to read for a law degree. He was still a student there in 1951 when he married Bombay-born Nusrat Isphahani.

Nusrat belonged to the first generation of her family to be born in what was then British-India. Her businessman father, Mirza Muhammad Abdul Latif Isphahani had his origins in the holy city of Najaf, now part of modern Iraq, and migrated to Bombay where he started his own soap-making business. Just before Partition the Isphahani family moved to Karachi and bought a house in the fashionable Clifton area, a stone's throw from where the Bhuttos would also build their family residence.

Zulfikar's ancestors were part of a completely different religious, business, and ethnic tradition. For a start they were Sunni Muslims, not Shias like the Isphahanis. They were rich, powerful landlords who owned thousands of acres of land in Sindh. Local Sindhi legend had it that you could roam the countryside on horseback for an entire day and never leave Bhutto-owned property. Mir Ghulam Murtaza Bhutto, Zulfikar's grandfather, is still remembered in Sindh for his love affair with an Englishwoman, the subsequent confiscation of his family property, and his enforced exile in neighbouring Afghanistan. He died at the age of 30, a month after his return to Larkana in 1899.

Zulfikar's father, Sir Shahnawaz, born in 1888, was politically active from an early age. He took charge of the family estates at the age of 21, was chosen as a leader of the Muslims of Sindh at the age of 25, and was elected to the Imperial Legislative Council in Delhi in 1919 at the age of 31. He was also president of the Larkana District Board until 1934 and a member of the Bombay Legislative Council until 1936. It was as a leader of the Sindhi Muslim community that he was invited to participate in the London Round Table Conferences on India between 1930 and 1933.

Zulfikar's biographer Stanley Wolpert wrote in *Zulfi Bhutto: His Life and Times*:

> The crowning achievement of Sir Shahnawaz's life was to convince Great Britain's rulers at the Round Table conference in London that Sindh deserved a separate provincial status, thus liberating his home from

Bombay, elevating sleepy Karachi overnight, once the Government of India Act of 1935 took effect, to equal status with other booming provincial capitals like Bombay, Calcutta and Madras. It was the single-most important economic-political coup won by an Indian Muslim since the founding of the Muslim League, eclipsed only by Quaid-e-Azam Jinnah's subsequent victory more than a decade later in winning his suit for separate nation-statehood for Pakistan.

Sir Shahnawaz would go on to become prime minister of Junagadh state, where he famously attempted and failed to secure the state's accession to Pakistan in 1947.

Zulfikar, born in 1928, was the youngest and only surviving male child of Sir Shahnawaz and his Hindu convert wife Khursheed Begum. He was just 29 years old when he was appointed a member of Pakistan's delegation to the United Nations. He was appointed a cabinet minister in charge of Energy when his daughter was 5 years old and he became foreign minister when she was 9.

Benazir was a 12-year-old boarder in 1965 at the Convent of Jesus and Mary in Murree when she first came face to face with the realities of war with India. As she chronicles in her autobiography *Daughter of the East* (1989):

> Where once we had played 'jacks' with goat bones after dinner, or read Enid Blyton books, now suddenly we had air raid practices and blackouts. The nuns made older girls responsible for getting their younger sisters into the shelters and I made Sunny [Sanam] tie her slippers to her feet at night so she wouldn't lose time in looking for them.

> Many of our schoolmates were daughters of prominent government officials or army officers, and with excitement we gave each other false names in case we fell into the hands of our enemies. In the flush of our adolescence, it was all quite dramatic, the possibility of being kidnapped and carried off into the hills. But for the seventeen days of war the threat of invasion was quite real and frightening.

Benazir was 13 when her father resigned from government, a year before he founded the Pakistan Peoples Party or PPP. Years later she would tell friends how she and her sister enthusiastically dipped into their pocket money to pay their subscriptions and join the long queue of people outside the family home in Karachi who wanted to join the new party. When Zulfikar was arrested and jailed for the first time by the military authorities in 1968, his daughter was preparing for secondary school 'O' level examinations. He wrote to her from prison:

> I am praying for your success in your 'O' level examinations. I am really proud to have a daughter who is so bright that she is doing O levels at the young age of fifteen, three years before I did them ... You have all the books you need. Read about Napoleon Bonaparte, the most complete man of modern history. Read about the American revolution ... Read about Bismarck and Lenin, Ataturk and Mao Tse-Tung. Read the history of India from ancient times. And above all read the history of Islam.

Benazir was Zulfikar and Nusrat's first child and her baby complexion was of such a rosy hue when she was born in Karachi on 21 June 1953 that she was immediately nicknamed Pinkie by her proud parents. Three other siblings followed in rapid succession, Mir Murtaza in 1954, Sanam in 1957, and Shahnawaz in 1958.

In the male-dominated Islamic culture prevalent in Pakistan, as Benazir herself repeatedly acknowledged, boys had traditionally been favoured over girls. Zulfikar was however a liberated man and his first born, notwithstanding her gender, attracted his tender affection, support, and interest from the outset. She was first sent to Lady Jennings nursery school in Karachi, then to a convent secondary school in the same city, followed by another convent for girls in Murree. Zulfikar always kept in close contact, often writing to praise her academic and other achievements, describing her as his jewel.

By the time Zulfikar was released from prison in 1969, Benazir had passed her 'O' level examination with flying colours and had been offered a place at Radcliffe College, Harvard. Her father's words of advice, chronicled in her autobiography, *Daughter of the East*, rang in her ears as she left for America:

> You will see many things that may surprise you in America and some that may shock you. But I know you have the ability to adapt. Above all you must study hard. Very few in Pakistan have the opportunity

et that
the money . . . . a debt to them, a
people who sweat an . . . . a debt to them, a
debt you can repay with God's blessing by using your education to better
their lives.

When Benazir crossed the Atlantic three years later and went on to
Oxford, her father's own alma mater, Zulfikar wrote to her:

> I feel a strange sensation in imagining you walking on the footprints I left
> behind at Oxford over twenty-two years ago. I was happy by your presence
> at Radcliffe but, since I was not at Harvard, I could not picture you there
> through the same camera. Here I see your presence like mine in flesh and
> blood, over every cobble of the streets of Oxford, over every step you take
> on the frozen step-ladders, through every portal of learning you enter.
>
> Your being at Oxford is a dream come true. We pray and hope that this
> dream turned into reality will grow into a magnificent career in the service
> of your people.

After she was elected president of the Oxford Union debating society,
she received a telegram of congratulations from her doting and evidently
proud father, 'Overjoyed at your election as President of the Oxford
Union, you have done splendidly. Our heart-warming congratulations
on your success, Papa.'

Like her sister and brothers, Benazir was from an early age exposed
to foreign VIPs with whom her father interacted, including such
statesmen as Chou En-lai and Henry Kissinger, but, being the eldest
child, she may have been more aware of the significance of the people
to whom she was introduced. When John F. Kennedy was shot in 1963,
10-year-old Benazir was travelling with her father in the provinces of
Pakistan. Although only dimly aware of Kennedy, she recalled how her
father woke her up, telling her this was no time to sleep because a great
tragedy had occurred. On another occasion she recalled the visit to her
Karachi home of a man who looked like Bob Hope, only to be gently
corrected by her mother who explained that the distinguished visitor was
actually the then US vice president Hubert Humphrey.

To further encourage his daughter's interest in foreign affairs,

Zulfikar took Benazir on two key foreign trips. The first was to New York in 1971, where the United Nations Security Council was meeting to discuss the India–Pakistan war. At the time Benazir was still an undergraduate at Harvard. In her autobiography, she tells of the abrupt message from her father summoning her to New York to be at his side while he tried to negotiate a ceasefire and the withdrawal of Indian forces from the then East Pakistan.

Six months later she was once again with him in the Indian summer resort of S[h]imla where India and Pakistan negotiated a peace pact following the end of the previous year's war. It was there that Benazir had her first taste of being treated as an international celebrity in her own right, and it was not just the attention she received from Indira Gandhi. On the streets of the city she was mobbed by cheering crowds, and every public statement, whether it concerned politics or fashion, was lapped up by the local and national Indian media. Even her astonished father was provoked to comment that his daughter must represent a diversion from the serious issues that were under discussion between the two delegations.

Two years later, in 1974, when Benazir was still at Oxford, Zulfikar arranged for her to fly back and be present at the Islamic summit conference he hosted in Lahore for the leaders of 38 Muslim countries, including Anwar Sadat from Egypt, King Feisal of Saudi Arabia, and Libya's Colonel Muammar Qadhafy. Returning to Oxford, she told her suitably impressed college friends of how she had met every single Islamic leader of any significance, ranging from the president of the .UAE to the emirs of Bahrain, Qatar, and Kuwait.

By the time she graduated from Oxford in 1976, Benazir was all set to fulfil her teenage ambition of joining Pakistan's Foreign Service, but, at her father's insistence, she stayed on at Oxford for an additional year to obtain a postgraduate qualification. She obtained her undergraduate degree in 1975 and stayed on for a postgraduate diploma. I had left Oxford by then.

Many children are close to their parents, but Benazir idolized her beloved 'Papa' and visibly basked in his affection. She was totally blind to his limitations and, as she demonstrated during her unsuccessful campaign to get him an honorary degree at Oxford, flew into a rage if anyone dared to suggest that Zulfikar was anything less than perfect.

Zulfikar certainly had his share of faults as a husband and father. A philanderer of legendary appetites, his affairs and mistresses were the talk of the town in Karachi. While he was a young cabinet minister in the Ayub Khan administration, long-suffering Nusrat was sufficiently provoked to seek a separation, pending a divorce, when the children were still toddlers.

He had no dearth of shortcomings too when it came to politics. History may well confer on Zulfikar the mantle of Pakistan's most popular ever elected leader. His Pakistan Peoples Party's slogan of '*roti, kapra, makan*' (food, clothes, shelter) went hand in hand with his avowedly socialist policies of nationalization and land distribution. These made him the darling of the masses from the time he assumed power in December 1971 until he was overthrown in a military coup in July 1977. He was in many ways a larger than life character whose fondness for Cuban cigars and Scotch whisky defied his country's Islamic customs and traditions. 'Yes, I drink alcohol,' he told one mass gathering in Lahore, 'but at least I don't drink the blood of the masses.'

However, his grand design for the transformation of the nature of Pakistani society hid some serious personal flaws. Although a democratically elected leader, he was a bully with authoritarian tendencies and intolerant of any opposition. Besides, the human rights record of his government in Baluchistan, where he sent in the army to crush what he believed was a secessionist movement, was appalling.

Notwithstanding his personal failings, the affection between father and daughter never waned. For one thing, Benazir was away abroad during the key years her father was in power and did not come face to face with the mounting criticism of his style of leadership. Perhaps it was also asking too much of a young and impressionable woman to take a step back and look with critical eyes at the father she adored. Inevitably, the father–daughter connection was strengthened and boosted between the time Zulfikar was arrested in July 1977, briefly freed, and re-arrested until the date of his execution in April 1979. During that period his wife and daughter were the only members of his immediate family who remained in Pakistan and had access to him as and when they were permitted by the military authorities.

Benazir herself wrote movingly of her visits, sometimes on her own and sometimes with her mother, first to Kot Lakhpat jail in Lahore and later to Rawalpindi Central Jail where Zulfikar was held until he was executed. Time after time she recorded the filthy conditions in which her father was held, the mosquito bites that covered his entire body, his bleeding gums, the vomiting of blood and, finally, his refusal to take any medication until he was led to the gallows.

Before Zulfikar's death Benazir and her mother were repeatedly detained in a cat and mouse game orchestrated by Zia. On the few occasions when she was free, Benazir was encouraged by her father to help sustain party morale by touring the country and, where possible, holding public meetings. Such meetings were however few and far between. More time was spent in helping to prepare Zulfikar's case in the Lahore High Court, which found him guilty in March 1978, and in the Supreme Court appeal that was rejected in February 1979.

Murtaza and Shahnawaz had been sent back abroad immediately after the coup, and from there they took responsibility for an international campaign to save their father's life. Benazir was in closer physical proximity to her father and in more regular contact but, and this was a big but, the rapport they sustained did not automatically translate into a mandate for Benazir to build a political career for herself as a future leader of the PPP and Zulfikar's nominated successor. In the immediate aftermath of Zulfikar's death, the burden of his legacy rested largely on the shoulders of his widow. When the opposition, including the PPP, united to form the Movement for the Restoration of Democracy (MRD), it was Nusrat to whom they looked in the first instance for leadership until she was allowed to go abroad for medical treatment in November 1982. Benazir, who stayed behind for the time being, spent most of her time in prison, some of it in solitary confinement and at other times under house arrest, until she too was freed on medical grounds and allowed to go into exile in January 1984. Significantly, Zulfiqar's last will and testament did not anoint Benazir as his immediate successor or even as a future leader of the PPP. Nearly 30 years later, when Benazir was assassinated, questions were asked about Benazir's will and whether she really did anoint her son as her successor.

At their last meeting in his cell in 1979, one day before he was hanged, Zulfikar told his wife, ' Give my love to the other children. Tell Mir and Sunny and Shah that I have tried to be a good father and wish I could have bade them good-bye.' Both Nusrat and Benazir were advised by him to leave Pakistan for their own peace of mind, but Nusrat told her husband, 'No. No. We can't go. We'll never go. The General must not think they have won. Zia has scheduled elections again, though who knows if he will dare to hold them? If we leave, there will be no one to lead the party; the party you built.'

Asked by her father if she would leave, Benazir replied, 'I could never go.' Zulfikar responded, 'I'm so glad. You don't know how much I love you; how much I've always loved you. You are my jewel; you always have been.' Many years after her father's death, Benazir was fond of quoting a letter he wrote her at the age of 15 when he was in prison and she was preparing for her high school 'O' Level examinations. Zulfikar said in his letter, 'I am really proud to have a daughter who is so bright ... At this rate you might become the President ...' Zulfikar's encouraging words, however, belied the facts. Pakistan was and remains a conservative Muslim country in which women are expected to take a back seat in the day-to-day business of running the country. It is far more likely that when it came to preserving and prolonging the Bhutto dynasty, Zulfikar had in mind his older son, Murtaza, a year younger than Benazir, but a son nevertheless who could campaign and win a political following in a way that a woman could not possibly hope to match.

To be fair to Benazir, she herself never anticipated a political career. At Oxford she repeatedly told friends of how she hoped to join the Pakistan Foreign Service, and it did not take much anticipation to forsee a glittering career for her as an influential and respected ambassador of her country. Indeed, it could be argued that Benazir took on her father's legacy and became prime minister by default. Had Zia not been killed in a plane crash, and if in the ensuing months leading up to elections Murtaza had not been barred from returning to Pakistan, the Bhutto family's history would have been very different.

True, during her years of exile in London, Benazir became a rallying point for the PPP opposition, but Murtaza and Shahnawaz were just as active in their own way in building up resistance to Zia and the other generals. They chose a military option by founding Al Zulfikar abroad and training their recruits to carry out acts of sabotage and assassination against the military regime. Shahnawaz subsequently died in mysterious circumstances in Cannes—suspected of being poisoned at Zia's behest —and Murtaza continued to stay away from his country for fear of being arrested and tried as a terrorist by the military authorities.

When martial law was lifted in December 1985, Benazir was the only member of the Bhutto family able and willing to return to the political arena. Sanam, her younger sister, had stayed out of politics, Shahnawaz was dead, Nusrat was still convalescing from her treatment for cancer, and Murtaza had no alternative but to stay abroad in exile. In Pakistan Zia would tell his cronies that he had committed an error by even allowing Benazir to return. Benazir herself was not quite certain what to expect when she did fly back in April 1986. She knew she had a following and that the army was unpopular. On the eve of her arrival in Lahore, party activists told her to expect a substantial welcoming crowd, but she and they were taken aback by the scale of her welcome.

Lahore was a small provincial airport in 1986 but, try as I might, I could not get physically close to Benazir as she emerged from the airport lounge. Outside the airport was a convoy of brightly decorated lorries, and as I wandered towards the top end of the queue, a voice shouted, 'Shyam'. The voice was that of Jehangir Masud, another Pakistani student from our Oxford days. I reached out for his hand and found myself in the lead lorry of the convoy conveying Benazir to Iqbal Park in Lahore's Minar-e-Pakistan. Jehangir and I stood behind her as the convoy wound its way slowly through the streets where the crowds were three and four deep.

Everywhere we went there were shouts of *Jiye Bhutto'* (long live Bhutto). Benazir herself said nothing, just concentrated on smiling and waving.

It was the first time I'd seen her at close quarters after Shahnawaz's mysterious death at Cannes the previous year. There was speculation in Cannes about a leather suitcase filled with US$100 bills sent by Zia that had been seen in the city, and the consensus among his friends and family was that Zia's agents had used the money to somehow get to him. Shahnawaz was the youngest of the Bhutto children and Benazir's favourite sibling. She addressed him by his pet name, Gogi, and was able to relate to him immediately when they met up in Cannes after seven years of separation.

After his death the military regime gave Benazir permission to take her brother's body back to Larkana for burial in the family graveyard. She was arrested soon afterwards and then released several weeks later to enable her to make a statement before the French court inquiring into Shahnawaz's death. No doubt she would have stayed away from Pakistan for at least the forseeable future, but martial law was unexpectedly lifted on 30 December 1985, paving the way for her triumphal return to Lahore.

The real surprise was the public meeting at Iqbal Park. The PPP had expected a few hundred thousand supporters to turn out for Benazir when in reality the crowd was estimated at about two million. Benazir's speech was short on substance but long on slogans. The crowd didn't mind. Mazhar Ali, the well-known Pakistani writer–editor and father of London-based left wing firebrand Tariq Ali, was beside me on the stage. From where we sat it was possible to feel the vibrations emanating from the crowd. *'Zia avey avey, ya Ziq javey, javey'* (should Zia stay or go), Benazir asked in her mix of Sindhi and Urdu. *'Javey, javey,'* the delighted crowd, roared back, fed up with the military crackdowns, floggings, and Islamic injunctions that had become a hallmark of the Zia regime. This was a very different Benazir from the tear-stained woman in black who sat on the floor of an apartment in London's Barbican complex, quietly sobbing in memory of Shahnawaz. As I watched her receive condolences from a never ending stream of supporters, it did not occur to me that she would be back in Pakistan less than a year later as the uncrowned queen of her country.

Indeed, if Benazir had any doubts about the depth of her support, they vanished after Lahore. She paid triumphal visits to her own home province of Sindh, as well as to the army heartlands of Punjab, prompting Zia to comment to the *New York Times* soon after Pakistan's Independence Day celebrations in August 1986, 'Miss Bhutto is not the problem. It is Miss Bhutto's unnecessary, impractical ambitions and her attitude towards acquiring power which are objectionable.'

Briefly arrested in 1986 and then released, Benazir's arranged marriage the following year was an occasion for yet more celebrations in Karachi and the rest of Sindh. Little was known about the bridegroom, Asif Zardari, except that he was a Sindhi from a landowning family and that his father owned Bambi cinema in Karachi. The troubling questions about his business dealings would come much later.

Benazir was six months pregnant with her son, Bilawal, when Zia tried to wrong-foot her by dissolving parliament in May 1988 and calling for elections. The election date was fixed for 16 November 1988, but Zia himself was unexpectedly killed three months earlier in August when his Lockheed C-130 aircraft crashed for reasons that have never been fully determined. The toxic gas bomb that caused the plane to crash was said to have been concealed in a crate of mangoes. Zia's 'insurance' against mid-air sabotage was American ambassador Arnold Raphel, but even Raphel's presence did not deter the still-to-be identified assassins.

Zia's grand plan to hold elections without named political parties was successfully challenged and overturned by Pakistan's Supreme Court. On 16 November the PPP and Benazir, by then the mother of a 2-month-old son, won a resounding victory. Just over two weeks later, on 2 December 1988, Zulfikar Ali Bhutto's daughter was sworn in as the first elected woman prime minister of the Muslim world and the fourth woman prime minister of the entire world after Srimavo Bandaranaike, Indira Gandhi, and Margaret Thatcher.

Benazir's moment of triumph, however, masked real problems she was facing with her surviving brother Murtaza. She was the more patient and pragmatic of the two, willing to endure the hardships of jail as the necessary price for the return of democracy to Pakistan. Murtaza was different. By 1988 he was a self-confessed hijacker and bomber who made several unsuccessful attempts to kill Zia. We met two months after his sister's inauguration when he told me how his agents had made five unsuccessful attempts to finish off the dictator, while he himself had survived six attempts against his own life.

The setting for our accidental encounter was the Sheraton Hotel in Damascus where I had been sent in February 1989 to await news about Terry Waite, the kidnapped personal envoy of the Archbishop of Canterbury. Waite had been kidnapped in neighbouring Lebanon, which had become a no-go area for foreign journalists. So, like the rest of my tribe, I chose to monitor negotiations for his release from across the mountains in Damascus. In the evening some of us were in the basement bar of the hotel, discussing the fate of Waite and other Western hostages, when Murtaza strode in. He was exactly the same as in our Oxford days, although the moustache was now somewhat bushier. 'Murtaza,' I called out. He stopped, put his hand into the right hand pocket of his red waistcoat and drew out a pearl-handled revolver. 'Who wants to know?' he responded. For a seemingly endless moment I was speechless. Then he laughed, 'Oh Shyam, I didn't recognize you; I have to be so careful.' Concerned at his state of mind, I retreated to my second floor hotel room. Half an hour later there was a banging on the door. 'Shyam, I'm sorry. Will you come down and play pool?' The more I resisted, the harder he knocked. I eventually relented and spent the next 11 hours until 6.00 in the morning talking to him in the pub/restaurant and pool room of the hotel.

The issue facing him was the consequence of his sister's election triumph and his willingness to stand trial or, better still, to use Benazir's good offices to obtain a pardon. Al Zulfikar, the terrorist organization that he and Shahnawaz had founded after their father's death, was after all an internationally proscribed group that had taken responsibility for the 1981 hijack of a Pakistan International Airlines aircraft on its way to Kabul. In the process one innocent Pakistani passenger, Captain Tariq Rahim, was erroneously identified as a key military target and shot dead. The other passengers were released after Zia agreed to release several dozen political prisoners, but not before commenting on the Bhutto brothers, 'We have thrown out the bad eggs and saved innocent lives.'

Was he willing to return to Pakistan to stand trial for the hijacking, I asked him. 'Yes,' Murtaza replied, but only if those military officers responsible for his father's death were first tried and hanged for treason. A decade after his father's death he was still consumed by a burning desire for revenge, and he claimed to have all the details of just what happened to Zulfikar on the night of his execution. As we talked into the night, a handful of Murtaza's friends drifted in and out of the room. Among them was his then Lebanese girlfriend, Ghinwa, later his wife, who Benazir subsequently, cruelly and contemptuously described as the 'Lebanese belly dancer'. 'He was never hanged,' Murtaza told me about his father. 'We saw the marks on his body: his face was like that of a young child. The eyes hadn't bulged, the lips had not turned purple. The back of his skull had been cracked by a pistol butt.'

Asked about Benazir and whether he wished he were in her place, Murtaza responded, 'I don't envy her. She has suffered by going to prison and has worked hard for it. After all, what good is power? It didn't save my father when the general killed him in his prison cell.' Several glasses of whisky later his mood changed, as did his previously charitable thoughts about his sister. He questioned her judgement in agreeing to form a government, saying, 'If it had been me I would have taken the PPP majority and gone into opposition ... having suffered so much, we could have suffered a little more. What I want to see is our people armed so that a military government is never allowed to capture power again.' He then repeatedly mocked Benazir with abusive five-letter words and worse, described her as an over-ambitious upstart who had usurped his rightful place as both prime minister and head of the Bhutto dynasty. 'I am the male; I should be prime minister,' he argued, before going on to insist that he was his father's chosen successor.

When the time came to test his assertion many years later after he returned to Pakistan, the response from the electorate was less than sympathetic. A popular election chant in 1993 in the Bhutto family's home province of Sindh was, 'Na Mir ka, na Pir ka, vote Benazir ka' (not for Mir [Murtaza] nor for Pir [Pir Pagara] vote only for Benazir). Murtaza advanced two arguments in support of his controversial claim. He was the one, not Benazir, who had been placed in charge of organizing his father's successful 1977 election campaign from Larkana constituency, and on the night of the coup it was he who was at his father's side when the soldiers stormed their home. 'Benazir and my mother were away in Karachi, so I went to wake papa,' Murtaza explained. Before being dragged away, Zulfikar told his older son, 'You must get out, I don't care how, by train, or plane, or camel.'

Two weeks after a toned down account of our conversation along with a picture was published in the Observer of London, I received a writ from Nusrat Bhutto accusing me of fabricating the interview in an attempt to embarrass her family. When I wrote back to her, insisting I was telling the truth, the writ was dropped. I had a witness to the interview. Some years later when I told Benazir the story of the writ, she said, 'Mir was Mummy's favourite—she wanted to protect him.' Few outside their immediate family knew of the bitterness and jealousy dividing Benazir and Murtaza as far back as 1989. Their differences deepened after he fought and won a seat in the Sindh provincial assembly while he was still abroad. After he finally returned home from exile in 1993, during Benazir's second term in office, he proclaimed himself the standard bearer of the PPP's true values as the party of the downtrodden, echoing his father's famous slogan of delivering bread, clothes, and homes to Pakistan's impoverished masses.

His impassioned pleas at a number of family gatherings fell on deaf ears as far as Benazir was concerned. He added insult to injury, however, by targeting her husband Asif Ali Zardari and holding him responsible for the charges of corruption that were being levelled against the PPP government. Nusrat, who sided with her son, suggested his appointment as chief minister of Sindh. An angry Benazir responded by expressing support for Abdullah Shah, a Zardari crony, who was the serving chief minister.

The family crisis worsened with public insults reportedly exchanged between Murtaza's and Shah's respective sets of followers. Soon after Murtaza and Zardari had their worst ever spat. One version has it that they were both flying first class from Rawalpindi to Karachi when Murtaza leant over and shaved off half of Zardari's moustache. The other more authoritative version is that Murtaza invited Zardari to his home with an offer to talk through and resolve their problems in private. When Zardari arrived, so this version goes, Murtaza's bodyguards grabbed him from behind and forcibly held him down while Murtaza personally shaved off half his moustache.

A few months later, Murtaza was returning to his Karachi home when he and his retainers were ambushed by 70 armed policemen, including four officers, who were lying in wait for them. When Murtaza got out of the car with his hands raised above his head, the police opened fire. Murtaza and seven others who were shot along with him were left bleeding on the street for nearly an hour before they were taken to hospital. Immediately after the shooting, all traces of the killing, including blood-stains, were wiped clean and any witnesses were either arrested or killed, including a policeman.

The widespread belief among horrified Pakistanis was that the decision to kill Murtaza had been taken at a very high level. Such suspicions were endorsed by a bitter Fatima Bhutto, Murtaza's daughter by his first wife, who related how the shot that killed her father had been fired execution-style at his neck. Fatima went on to say that none of the police officers involved in the shooting were arrested. Instead, all the witnesses and survivors were arrested, two later dying in police custody. Fatima's account of how she tried to reach her aunt at the time was reported by renowned Pakistani author and left wing campaigner

Tariq Ali. In his article published in the *London Review of Books* in December 2007, Ali relates how Fatima made contact with Zardari at the prime minister's house and asked to speak to Benazir. Zardari responded by saying it was not possible, adding, 'She's hysterical, can't you hear?' Asked why, Zardari responded, 'Don't you know? Your father's been shot.'

3

THE MARRIAGE BUSINESS

ZULFIKAR HAD BEEN DEAD AND BURIED FOR EIGHT YEARS, SHAHNAWAZ FOR TWO, AND THERE WAS CONSTANT bickering with Murtaza in the background when Benazir astonished her friends in the West by agreeing to an arranged marriage. Whether she was motivated by the loss of her father and brother, or the never-ending sense of political and family isolation, or a combination of both we shall never know. Speaking to a reporter from the *Los Angeles Times* shortly before the wedding, she commented, 'I don't really expect people in the West to understand. Every mother wants her daughter married and I felt obligations to my family and my religion.' On another occasion she inquired, in another famously quoted remark about arranged marriages, 'Really, how is it any different from using a computer dating service?'

In her autobiography, *Daughter of the East*, she claims that an arranged marriage was the price in personal choice she had to make because her high profile precluded meeting a suitable partner in the normal course of daily life. Her one concession to modernity was the instruction she issued to her mother to pay no dowry. Later in the book she confesses to feeling lonely and reasoning with herself that in the male, chauvinistic society of Pakistan remaining single would work against her. It was another way of saying that marriage was a political necessity and an arranged marriage was the price she would have to pay if she was aiming for high office in such a conservative country. It was also probably true that because of her political life she would find it difficult to enjoy a normal courtship culminating in a love marriage. On the other hand, she had considered marriage when still a student at Oxford and had been turned down by the men of her choice.

There was of course no dearth of other Pakistani men who saw her as a great prize and would queue up for her hand. One was the son of a senior party functionary, but he was believed to have a drink problem. Another party loyalist was also turned down by her because he came across as an opportunist, although he did win favour in a different way some years later when he was brought into the cabinet. Choosing a consort for the prime minister, Pakistani friends would laughingly tell me, is somewhat akin to the prime minister choosing the army commander-in-chief. The future husband, like the army commander, has to be reliable, loyal, incorruptible, and willing to play second fiddle to the boss.

Asif Ali Zardari appeared to fulfil all those requirements. He was a fellow Sindhi, the son of cinema owner Hakim Ali Zardari and his wife Zarin. His only apparent vice, if it could be called that, was a passion for polo. Pakistani contemporaries recall his penchant for stylish Gucci-type clothes, expensive wristwatches, and sleek foreign cars. Described by others as a man of limited wealth and limited education, the younger Zardari was said to have been selected by Nusrat as her daughter's spouse. Sent by his father to Pakistan's Cadet College Petaro near Hyderabad, a finishing school for wannabe soldiers, followed by a few months spent at a London commercial college, his educational pedigree was no match for Benazir's. Under Pakistan's un-amended election rules, his lack of a university degree also meant he was not qualified to stand for election to the National Assembly. Thus, although anointed with his son as co-chair of the PPP following Benazir's assassination, existing legislation blocked his immediate transition to the position of prime minister.

On the eve of her wedding, when she had all her body hair plucked, Benazir was the first to admit that they 'didn't really love each other yet', although that would change soon after the formal exchange of nuptials. Soon after their wedding the happy couple travelled to London where Zardari told a gathering of friends how his parents had gifted them a three-bedroom apartment in the city's fashionable Campden Hill Gardens. Benazir, who was present, piped up from the background, 'Yes darling, but they have also given us their mortgage.' 'He's been very good to me,' Benazir said later in a *BBC* interview. 'If someone is good to you, you respond to that. Secondly, he's a very honourable person. I have tremendous respect for him and that's another good foundation for a marriage.'

Bilawal, their son, was born two months before the elections that propelled her into office. Once she was prime minister it is fair to assume that father and son each vied for her attention, in competition with the daily affairs of state with which she was expected to deal. Friends recall that notwithstanding the pressures of her job, she was a woman in bloom, and Zardari was always there to provide whatever support was needed. During her second term Zardari was appointed a cabinet minister, as was Nusrat, prompting the joke that very soon Bilawal too would be given the portfolio, in all likelihood as minister for children's affairs.

One minister in her government recalled the cabinet meetings when Benazir and Zardari were like two lovebirds billing and cooing at each other across the table. He used the analogy of the popular Layla-Majnun love story, hugely popular in India and Pakistan, to describe the way they interacted with each other, even in public. The scandals involving corruption and money-laundering began emerging soon after. Those allegations focused mostly on Zardari, implying that he was using his marriage to cement lucrative business deals, although it was widely alleged that the couple between them accumulated over US$1 billion.

When he was first arrested in 1990, shortly after his wife's government was dismissed, the charge against Zardari was blackmail. He was alleged to have tied a remote-controlled bomb to the leg of a UK-based Pakistani businessman, Murtaza Bukhari, before sending him into a bank to withdraw money from his account. The case was dropped in 1993 when Benazir returned to power a second time and her husband was freed from prison. As these stories about Zardari circulated in Pakistan and abroad, it was ironic that Benazir failed to heed her own father's warnings about how those in power and their families needed to be extra careful when it came to issues of money and lifestyle. Back in 1978, at Zulfikar's request, Benazir wrote to Murtaza in New York, stating:

> Caesar's wife must be above suspicion. The Press here has said you are living lavishly in London which Papa knows you are not, but he wants me to remind you that your personal life must be most circumspect. No films, no extravagance, or people will say you are enjoying yourself while your father languishes in a death cell.

In 1994, a senior British diplomat, aware of my association with Benazir, took me aside and told me how he had cast-iron proof that Zardari was receiving kickbacks on certain Pakistani defence deals. He said he had asked for a face-to-face meeting with Benazir, and at this he told her all he knew. She listened without commenting, then turned her face away until he left the room.

Benazir and I exchanged messages but did not meet while she was prime minister. When we did finally meet again in Dubai for a detailed discussion in 2003, seven years after she was removed from office for the second time, there were stories flying around all over the world about corruption and shady deals linked to her husband. That was the year when a Swiss judge, Daniel Devaud, formally convicted Benazir, Zardari, and family legal adviser Jens Schlegelmilch of money-laundering, ordering them to return US$11 million to the Pakistani government. The appeal against that conviction was due to be heard in 2008.

The Pakistan government's British lawyer, Jeremy Carver, told the media after the 2003 judgement:

When the judge finally makes his determination on this after years of trying to delay the whole proceedings which came basically from Benazir's lawyers, he makes a determination that convicts Schlegelmilch, Bhutto, Zardari for money-laundering.

He orders the restitution to the state of Pakistan of $11 million approximately that was still frozen in bank accounts in Switzerland. Judge Devaud has been asked subsequently if he has any doubts about it, the findings that he made. And he says absolutely no, it's an open and shut case.

The most damning judgement of all was delivered by Fatima Bhutto in a now famous opinion piece written for the *Los Angeles Times* two weeks before Benazir died. Describing her aunt as the twice-disgraced former prime minister, Fatima went on to say:

It is widely believed that Ms Bhutto lost both her governments on grounds of massive corruption. She and her husband, a man who came to be known in Pakistan as 'Mr 10%', have been accused of stealing more than $1 billion from Pakistan's treasury. She is appealing a money-laundering conviction by the Swiss courts involving about $11 million. Corruption cases in Britain and Spain are ongoing.

Judge Devaud first indicted Zardari and Benazir on the money-laundering charges in 1998. Long before that there were equally scandalous claims made in Pakistan of how Zardari had bought a multi-million pound country estate, Rockwood, which comprised 365 acres of prime land in Surrey. Shortly before Benazir's government was dismissed in 1996, opposition leader Nawaz Sharif gave a detailed description of Rockwood to parliament in Islamabad. He described it as a palace 10 times larger than the magnificent Lahore fort built centuries earlier by the Mughal emperors of India.

Nawaz's accusations were followed up two years later in 1998 by a series of investigative articles in the *New York Times*, entitled, 'Bhutto Clan Leaves Trail of Corruption in Pakistan'. The author of the articles, staff reporter John Burns, drew on what were described as a cache of family documents, including bank statements that detailed payments made into accounts listed in the names of Zardari and Nusrat. Burns said Benazir's personal involvement in the financial wheeling and dealing he uncovered was uncertain, but he went on to list a vast collection of questionable financial transactions with which Zardari was associated. These included a US$10 million deposit paid into one of Zardari's accounts from a gold bullion dealer in the Gulf who had been given a monopoly by the Bhutto government to import gold into Pakistan. The documents also listed a US$200 million commission that French military contractor Dassault Aviation agreed to pay Zardari for a US$4 billion jet fighter deal that fell apart at the last minute. Zardari was also recorded as going on an expensive international shopping spree to buy exotic jewellery and the controversial Rockwood estate. The newspaper cited Pakistani investigators uncovering a string of luxury apartments in London and a country club and polo ranch in Florida linked to the Bhutto family. It also reported the negligible tax returns filed by Nusrat, Zardari, and Benazir during her years in office, with no listing of any foreign bank accounts or properties held which Pakistani law required them to reveal. Benazir's highest declared income was US$42,200 in 1996 with US$5,110 in tax. Zardari declared no net assets at all in 1990, the end of Benazir's first term, and only US$402,000 in 1996.

After Benazir's death, Burns filled me in on the backdrop to his investigations. Zardari was in prison in Karachi when Burns showed up to ask for his reactions to the documents in his possession. Zardari studied them for 10 minutes before reacting. 'I don't need to look at them, I have the originals; these are from our files,' he told the *NY Times* reporter. Burns then went to see Benazir, then the leader of the opposition. When he told her of the evidence he had collected and Zardari's response, she broke down sobbing: 'Why are you doing this to me,' she asked. 'After all that's happened to my family, my father killed, my brothers killed.'

I had read the *NY Times* articles before I sat down to dinner with Benazir in Dubai in 2003, but as I hadn't had a lengthy personal interaction for some years my aim was to avoid a cops and robbers style media interrogation which made her feel cornered and react accordingly. Nevertheless, as I started our taped question and answer session, Rockwood was the first name that came to my lips. Benazir was evasive in her replies. 'I did not buy Rockwood, I have never visited Rockwood, and if I accept the accusation that he bought Rockwood, where is the illegality?' she asked. Commenting about her husband's work, she added, 'He was a businessman, he had money, there were bearer certificates, he was permitted to remit his money overseas to international tax shelters. He was allowed to put his money in an international tax shelter legally. So did Mr James Goldsmith,' she added, referring to the English billionaire and founder of the English Referendum Party.

The dig at Goldsmith was deliberate. He had agreed to investigate Zardari's overseas holdings at the behest of his daughter Jemima who was married to former Pakistan test cricketer and aspiring politician Imran Khan. Benazir and Imran had been friendly at Oxford but as adults they rarely saw eye to eye. Jemima couldn't stand Benazir either, describing her as a 'kleptocrat in a Hermes headscarf', adding that her terms in office were marked by 'incompetence, exra judicial killings, and brazen looting'.

Quoting her husband's own denial of financial impropriety (how can anyone think of buying a mansion in England when people in Pakistan don't even have a roof over their heads), Benazir took the opportunity to slam Pakistan's military ruler, saying, 'may I ask General Musharraf what properties he has? He's taken huge amounts of commercial property, agricultural property. He's taken houses for himself ... where does he get his money from?' Pervez Musharraf had by then been in power for four years after overthrowing the elected civilian government headed by Benazir's rival, Nawaz Sharif. He was the military ruler who said after his coup that he would fight tooth and nail to prevent either Benazir or Nawaz from ever returning to power.

Meanwhile I reminded Benazir about what her father had said about Caesar's wife and how in the tradition of Caesar's wife a spouse of someone in high office had not only to be clean but be seen to be so. She replied, saying of her husband:

> Yes, if he was my cabinet minister. He was my cabinet minister for three months. Of course if he was my cabinet minister and he did something, it would be abuse of office. But Rockwood is not purchased according to the

court papers in the three months that he was a cabinet minister and, under Pakistani law, people who are members of the National Assembly have private practices—they practise law, they practise medicine, they do their trading, they sell commodities, they buy commodities, they do consultancies. There is no illegality involved.

Almost a year to the day of our Dubai interview, Zardari did a U-turn and admitted that the controversial £4.5 million estate belonged to him. Rockwood had been put up for sale and the Pakistan government was claiming its share of the proceeds when Zardari's lawyer appeared before the judge to say that his client was the 'beneficial' owner of the property. In truth it had always been difficult for Zardari to deny he was Rockwood's proprietor. To begin with, his children went horse-riding in its grounds. Soon after the property had been purchased Zardari visited the local pub, the Dog & Pheasant, and tried to purchase it because he liked it so much. When told it was not for sale, he said he would build an exact replica of it in Rockwood's basement. Then there was the testimony of a local builder, Paul Keating, who told the media how he had seen crates arriving from Pakistan stuffed with antique rifles, carpets, and furniture, including a 30-ft long cut-glass dining table, a stuffed tiger, statues, and several oil paintings. A furniture supplier called Sarosh Yaqub Mehi later told investigators how she sent 80 pieces to the Pakistan High Commission in London, apparently destined for Zardari's use in Rockwood, and was bound to confidentiality. 'I was hushed up,' she said. Keating was personally recruited by Zardari to implement modifications to the estate, which came with a helipad, indoor swimming pool, a nine hole golf course, and paddock. Its other attractions included marble bathrooms, copper-clad doors, and a master bedroom suitably modified with reinforced walls to protect against bombs. Hundreds of fibre-optic lights were fitted into the ceiling of the master bedroom to mimic a starry sky.

Looking back now, Benazir's evasive responses to the Rockwood inquiry cast a question mark over her answers to several other equally controversial allegations. The most serious of these was that both husband and wife benefited from illegal commissions from Swiss companies appointed to carry out customs investigations of goods being sent to Pakistan. 'The charge is a simple one,' Benazir told me. 'The charge is that Benazir Bhutto abused her position as prime minister of Pakistan to influence the awards of the pre-shipment contracts to financially benefit her husband.' Unsurprisingly, she rejected the accusation.

It was Sharif in opposition and then the administration of General Pervez Musharraf that focused on overseas bank accounts in the British Virgin Islands and Switzerland that were said to process the black money earned from illegal commissions. The investigations initiated by Sharif were augmented in 1996 by Sir James Goldsmith who used private investigators to uncover several accounts in London and Switzerland, as well as property in the UK and France, that were linked to Zardari. In 2003, a Swiss court identified one company in particular, Bomer Finance, registered in the British Virgin Islands, of which Zardari was described as the beneficial owner. The court was told that commissions worth US$8.2 million were paid into Bomer and how Benazir was the only person to access the funds before they were frozen. Bomer excited public interest for another reason, which was that it was money from this account that Benazir was alleged to have used to purchase a £117,000 diamond necklace from an upmarket jewellery store in London's fashionable Knightsbridge. Benazir flatly denied all knowledge of the necklace, claiming she had been framed in the manner of Marie Antoinette, the wife of Louis XVI of France. Between gales of laughter she told me:

> This necklace—if it was mine—it would be with me. But it reminds me of Marie Antoinette ... she was trapped because there was a woman who wore a gown like Marie Antoinette and took this very expensive necklace and pretended that the Queen had bought it. And when it went to trial it was found that the Queen hadn't bought it. But you know women are associated with necklaces. So the necklace makes it a human story and it makes people focus on the necklace rather than on the dry account of Bomer. So this is where the necklace comes in.

Some of the documentation relating to the overseas bank accounts was alleged to have come from the office of Geneva lawyer Jens Schlegelmilch, described in media reports as the Bhutto family's agent in Europe. Distancing herself from Schlegelmilch, Benazir told me:

> He is the man who established the offshore accounts [bank accounts] and operated them and he is somebody who has an Irani wife and through his Irani wife befriended my mother along with many others when she was living in Geneva. But he has never acted as my agent in the past, present or any time. He has never been given power of attorney or anything to act on my behalf.

As for Zardari, he continued to deny all allegations of improper financial dealings, notwithstanding the new information that emerged about Rockwood and Judge Devaud's ruling. Shortly after he was released from prison in 2004, he agreed to a series of interviews with Pakistani journalists to put the record straight. Typical was his early 2005 session with journalist and film producer Beena Sarwar, who published her interview with him on the Internet website *Chowk*. They haven't proved one case against me,' Zardari told her.

> You know how it started? It was Gen. Mujibur Rehman's brainchild [former information minister during the Zia ul Haq regime], to use the old trick: give the dog a bad name and hang him. So they created this image of me as an Achilles heel of PPP. I couldn't counter it because I didn't have a political image. I did have a personal political history, my family has always been in politics that people chose to ignore, but prison was a new experience for me. History will redeem me. What am I? I am just a bleep in the universal picture. So I might as well try and shine.

4

A STARTLING REVELATION

INTENSE DISCUSSIONS ABOUT ZARDARI, THE OFFSHORE BANK ACCOUNTS, AND THE DIAMOND NECKLACE HAD LEFT both of us exhausted. Therefore, when Benazir suggested we take a break and have dinner cooked by her staff in the Dubai villa, I willingly agreed.

We moved to the middle of the large front room where she received her guests. On one side were the sofas and armchairs, and on the other a long dining table around which she sometimes held discussions with her PPP advisers. At the far corner was a door which I understood led to the suite of rooms assigned to Nusrat. 'Will your mother be joining us?' I asked. Benazir shook her head, 'She's much too sick; she'll find it difficult just to sit down with us.' Later she explained how Nusrat had contracted a form of Alzheimer's and how her poor physical condition was aggravated by the beatings meted out to her by Zia's security personnel. There was no mention of past mother–daughter tensions over Murtaza.

As we talked, her Pakistani servants brought in the food. Before I knew it, the table was awash with bowls of fresh fruit, separated by other bowls of chocolate ice cream and interspersed with huge oval dishes of lamb and chicken biriyani. 'I'm sorry that's all there is today,' said Benazir in a half-apologetic tone. By then the children had been whisked off to bed and we had just begun eating when she suddenly asked me why I thought the Pakistani military seemed to have it in for her. Caught completely off guard, I mumbled something about male chauvinism, adding that in their benighted way the men in uniform probably thought she was not up to the job of prime minister.

There was pin-drop silence. 'Well let me tell you something,' Benazir declared with her eyes narrowing, 'I have done more for my country than all the military chiefs of Pakistan combined.' There was something so deliberate and serious in her tone that I put down my knife and stopped eating, so that I could listen more closely. As I looked up, she told me to ensure that my tape-recorder was switched off so that she could let me in on a secret. This secret, she went on, was so significant that I had to promise never to reveal it, at least not during her lifetime. Not knowing what to expect, I nodded, extracted the tape-recorder from my pocket and placed it with its switch turned off in front of her.

'You know I cannot take credit for our nuclear programme, that goes to my father,' Benazir started, pausing momentarily at that stage for greater effect, 'but I am the mother of the missile programme.' I was totally baffled. I knew a little bit about nuclear weapons development— my research at Oxford had been about the origins of India's nuclear programme—but I knew next to nothing about missiles. Of course, like anyone interested in South Asia, I had read media reports about India's indigenously produced Prithvi range of short range rockets (up to 350 km range) that had been test-fired in the 1980s. The Prithvi was not some isolated Indian achievement, but part of an integrated space research and satellite-launch programme. Thus the Prithvi, the Akash surface-to-surface missile, the shorter range Trishul, the satellite launch vehicle space booster, and the Rohini range of satellites were all part of this planned development. The longer range Agni, capable of hitting all Pakistan's population centres, was first test-fired in 1989, and it was the development of this variant, Benazir inferred, that had caused most concern amongst Pakistan's defence scientists. When she came into office for the second time in 1993 there were agonized discussions underway about how Pakistan could augment and strengthen its existing missile capabilities.

Short range rockets, the Hatf series, had been developed with French help in the mid-1980s, but they were considered to be of battlefield range only. The Chinese stepped in with the longer range, solid fuel M-9 and M-11 rockets, but even these were no match for India's steady progress with the Agni under the leadership of Professor Abdul Kalam, who would in later years become India's ceremonial president. What the Pakistanis desperately needed and sought was a launch platform for their own nuclear warheads that could match, perhaps even surpass, the delivery capability that India was developing. China could have helped, but Beijing was a signatory of the Missile Technology Control Regime, which restricted the technology it could transfer to Islamabad. To complicate matters further, Pakistan's own scientists could not agree on whether to concentrate all their efforts on further developing the solid propellant missiles acquired from China, or the liquid propellant variety that could conceivably be bought from North Korea. Eventually it was decided to pursue both types in parallel with each other, even though this was likely to encourage feuds and jealousies among rival groups of Pakistani scientists.

The North Koreans had a reactor and reprocessing plant from which they had managed to extract enough plutonium to manufacture one or two bombs by 1990. However, faced with mounting international pressure to shut down their plutonium facilities, North Korean scientists were looking for ways to develop a parallel uranium enrichment programme that would be free from the prying eyes of the international community. Pakistan was ideally placed to help because of the enrichment secrets that A.Q. Khan, the Dutch-trained metallurgist, had stolen from European laboratories, and who so impressed Zulfikar with his boast that Pakistan could match and even surpass India as South Asia's leading nuclear weapons state. Khan's success in stealing the secrets of uranium enrichment from top secret European laboratories laid the basis for Pakistan's own enrichment programme at the Kahuta Research Laboratories (KRL) outside Islamabad. Later Khan and colleagues from the Pakistani scientific community would become regular visitors to North Korea. By 1998 there were nine military flights a month ferrying military officers and scientists between Islamabad and Pyongyang.

In 1993 the central question was how the enrichment for missiles barter could be effected. Pakistan was under the spotlight as it had never been before, with India, Russia, and the secret services of the West monitoring every nuance of the country's military research. This was where Benazir came in useful. As she was due to visit North Korea at the end of 1993 she was asked and readily agreed to carry critical nuclear data on her person and hand it over on arrival in Pyongyang. The link with Pyongyang had been forged 22 years earlier by Zulfikar when he bought conventional arms from North Korea in 1971. Later, Pakistani and North Korean engineers are said to have worked together as joint advisers to develop Iran's rockets. North Korean leader Kim Il Sung acknowledged the family connection when he welcomed Benazir to the Kumsusan Assembly hall in Pyongyang, praising her father who had worked so assiduously to consolidate bilateral ties.

Much of what Benazir told me that evening I committed to memory, as I was not permitted to take notes or make use of my tape-recorder. We had got to the dessert stage and were nibbling away at a tray of fresh fruits when she came out with the big secret. The gist of what she told me was that before leaving Islamabad she shopped for an overcoat with the 'deepest possible pockets' into which she transferred CDs containing the scientific data about uranium enrichment that the North Koreans wanted. She did not tell me how many CDs were given to her to carry, or who they were given to when she arrived in Pyongyang, but she implied with a glint in her eye that she had acted as a two-way courier, bringing North Korea's missile information on CDs back with her on the return journey. Pakistani contacts later explained that Benazir returned with more than just CDs. The delighted North Koreans, who had already sold missiles technology to Egypt, Iraq, Libya,

Syria, and Yemen insisted she carry back the disassembled parts of an entire missile, the Nodong, so that Pakistani scientists could study it part by part in the security of their own laboratories. The Nodong was based on the Scuds that Egypt acquired from the Soviet Union before the 1973 Middle East war. When Egypt later sold the Scuds to Pyongyang, North Korean scientists reverse-engineered them to produce the Nodong.

Both to me and others, on the record at a later date, Benazir changed her story to insist that the Nodong was a strictly cash deal. 'So I took it up with Kim Il Sung … he agreed … and it was cash; they needed money and so it was done for cash.' In fact the cost of purchasing the first dozen Nodongs was estimated at a massive three billion dollars, and with Pakistan short of cash the speculation at the time was that Islamabad and Pyongyang had agreed a barter deal to exchange uranium enrichment technology for missiles. Benazir's visit thus certainly paved the way for scientists and military officers to start travelling between Pyongyang and Islamabad. Pakistan never convincingly denied reports that North Korean scientists were present when Islamabad carried out its nuclear tests in 1998. Just prior to the 1998 tests, North Korean defector Hwang Jang-yop, a former aide to Kim Il Sung, testified to the existence of a secret deal between Islamabad and Pyongyang to exchange long range missiles for enrichment technology.

To say that I was taken by surprise by Benazir's disclosure in Dubai would be a huge under-statement. The idea of the Pakistani prime minister acting as a female James Bond was simply incredible. Why she chose to tell me, albeit with my promise to keep it a secret during her lifetime, I will never know. I did keep my promise, but the information given to me kept buzzing around in my head and was responsible for keeping me awake all night long. Six months later in London Benazir agreed to do another detailed interview on the record, this time about Pakistan's nuclear programme, and I thought this was an opportunity to get her to repeat the North Korean story on tape. Sadly, try as I might, she would not play. If anything, the off-the-record story had changed.

In the newer, vaguer version the notorious A.Q. Khan, Pakistan's uranium enrichment expert, had asked her to somehow get hold of North Korea's missile technology from Kim Il Sung.

'I talked to him [Kim], he agreed,' Benazir told me on the record. '... it was done for cash. It was to be given to us in instalments of computer discs.' 'But,' I protested, 'you told me you carried it in your pocket; you told me off the record then. You told me not to use it and I never did.' Conscious that months earlier she may have told me more than she had intended, a flustered, Benazir replied on the record with the tape running, 'Okay, thank you. I didn't carry it—it symbolically, symbolically.' I pressed on, asking if it was details of the North Korean Nodong that Pakistan acquired. Benazir replied, 'I don't know what is Nodong ... we have improvised Scuds that were used in Afghanistan, we have shorter MII missiles, which we [the PPP] call the Zulfikar and they [the army] call the Ghauri. And then in '93 we did the agreement to get the missile technology which was delivered to us—'94/'95—on those computer disks.'

5

THE AMERICAN CONNECTION

IN 1989 BENAZIR HAD EVERY REASON TO BE PLEASED WITH THE SUDDEN, POSITIVE CHANGES IN HER PERSONAL AND professional life. A mother-to-be and an elected prime minister at the age of 35, the first ever woman prime minister of a Muslim country, she could celebrate and commemorate the memory of her dead father and former prime minister who had been hanged only 20 years earlier for a crime he insisted he did not commit.

She also, however, realized that much of what she had succeeded in achieving at the political level would not have been possible without the active support of a former student and family friend, an American, whose decisive interventions over the previous few years had been instrumental in freeing her from jail and later, following the 1988 elections, securing her the post of prime minister. The importance of the right American connection for someone like Benazir could scarcely be over-stated. Eight months after Zulfikar's death in 1979, Soviet troops entered Afghanistan, and neighbouring Pakistan became a frontline state for proxy US attacks on the occupying forces. From then on all that mattered in Pakistan was what the Americans wanted.

For Zia, the Soviet invasion was a godsend. Until then, given his treatment of Zulfikar and Pakistan's covert nuclear weapons programme, he had been viewed as an international pariah with a limited political life. After the Soviet occupation everything changed. As US military and financial aid poured into Pakistan, Zia became Washington's best friend against communist expansionism. The right wing Reagan administration was not interested in Zia's domestic policies, or how he handled his political opponents at home. All that mattered was his willingness to stand up and be counted as the West's ally against Moscow. Zia permitted the CIA to train and arm the anti-Soviet mujahiddin who took refuge in Pakistan. He and other Pakistani leaders, including Benazir, also colluded in training the future Taliban.

Inevitably, the importance of Deane Hinton or Robert Oakley, the US ambassadors in Islamabad in those years, was boosted beyond the expectations of either the Pakistanis or the Americans themselves. Between the 1979 invasion and the 1988 Geneva Accords that saw the Soviet Union withdraw, they acted as bankers, sheriffs, and best friends combined for the Pakistani government. Cynics in Islamabad took note of how the US ambassador was invited to attend meetings of the army corps commanders and even the cabinet. The joke in the Pakistani capital was that the American ambassador was actually a viceroy in disguise and should be treated accordingly.

By the same token, any Pakistani with influential friends in Washington could be expected to rely on them for some minimal protection from Zia's excesses. This was certainly true for Benazir, and in her case she was especially fortunate that the American with whom she maintained contact long after leaving university became a key player in the making of American foreign policy. His name was Peter Galbraith, one of the three sons of the renowned US economist and former ambassador to India John Kenneth Galbraith, whose loyal friendship played a key role in helping Benazir achieve her political goals.

Benazir and Galbraith first met as children in 1962 when visiting US First Lady Jacqueline Kennedy attended a horse show in the Pakistani border city of Lahore. Her escort was Galbraith's father, then the US ambassador to India, who took his family along with him for the trip across the border. Waiting to receive them at the other end was Zulfikar Ali Bhutto, then the foreign minister of Pakistan, and a long time admirer of the economist-turned diplomat. Zulfikar, 20 years younger, was an avid reader of Galbraith's works and had been in contact with him during his student days at the University of California.

When Benazir was admitted to Radcliffe College, Harvard, in 1969, Zulfikar asked the Galbraiths—he was by then professor of economics at Harvard—to act as his daughter's local guardians. In her memoirs Benazir comments on her reactions to meeting Peter at his parents' home shortly before term started, reacting negatively in private to his cigarette smoking, long hair, and unkempt clothes. She goes on to write, 'Little did I know then the role Peter ... would play in my release from detention in Pakistan 15 years later.'

On the surface the two of them had little in common. She had led a cloistered and privileged life as the daughter of Pakistan's foreign minister and later prime minister. The schools she attended, including the convent in the hills of Murree, were like little oases isolated from the rough and tumble of everyday life. Galbraith also came from a privileged background. As the son of John Kenneth Galbraith, he was part of America's intellectual élite but, unlike Benazir, he was more exposed to the realities of the outside world. Whether participating in student protests, or simply enjoying his personal freedom as an above average white American male, his was a world several times removed from that of Benazir. Nevertheless, perhaps because of the family connection, they kept up their association. When Benazir followed Galbraith to Oxford, he was at the very least a familiar face on whom she could rely. He would in time become a key supporter in Benazir's election campaign for the Oxford Union, helping her, for example, by co-hosting parties to attract the support of student voters.

After Oxford, Galbraith went on to Georgetown University in Washington DC where he secured a law degree before taking on a staff job with the Senate Foreign Relations Committee. He worked for Senate minority leader Claiborne Pell of Rhode Island and later became one of the Committee's South Asia experts. In 1993, President Bill Clinton appointed him US ambassador to Croatia.

As Benazir would later discover, Galbraith became one of her most influential and important supporters in Washington. He campaigned on her behalf behind the scenes and, given the nature of his job, was able to maintain contact with key senators and congressmen who were persuaded to look sympathetically at her cause. When the PPP emerged as the single largest political party in the 1988 elections, Galbraith was at Benazir's side, advising her what to say and do as she waited for her all-important call from Zia's successor inviting her to form the next government. Like so many of Benazir's friends at Harvard and Oxford, Galbraith was shocked by Zulfikar's execution and appalled by the tribulations suffered by his wife and daughter. Unlike many of the rest of us, he tried to see them when he could and used his contacts to press for their release.

When 1 first visited Pakistan in December 1983, I managed to smuggle a handwritten note through mutual friends to Benazir in her Karachi home, 70 Clifton. Later, when I was given access to Zia, I would use our interviews to ask after her and always received the same blank response that only changed when she was allowed to return to Pakistan from exile in August 1986.

Both Benazir and Nusrat were imprisoned for six months after Zulfikar's death, then held under house arrest for a further six months before being released in April 1980. They were re-arrested in March 1981 following the launch of the opposition parties' Movement for the Restoration of Democracy, known as MRD. The immediate pretext for arresting Zulfikar's widow and older daughter was the hijacking of a PIA jet by Kabul-based militants of the Al Zulfikar resistance movement headed by Benazir's brothers Murtaza and Shahnawaz. Nusrat was released on health grounds from Karachi jail in July 1981, but there was no relief for Benazir. Locked up first in Karachi, then in Sukkur prison in the remote Sindh desert, and back again in Karachi, she suffered prolonged periods of solitary confinement. Galbraith sprang into action when Benazir was in solitary confinement in Sukkur. He was the South Asia expert for the Senate Foreign Relations Committee and visited Pakistan in August 1981 to review US security interests.

Although carrying a letter from Senator Claiborne Pell requesting access, the Pakistani authorities refused to let Galbraith visit Benazir. The best he could manage was lunch at the Karachi Boat Club with Nusrat and Sanam where he handed them a long personal letter for Benazir. Although denied access to Benazir, Galbraith used the experience of his trip to prepare a report for the Foreign Relations Committee. His report argued for a more forceful human rights policy and warned that the imminent resumption of US economic and military assistance to Islamabad risked identifying Washington with an unpopular military dictatorship.

There was little prospect of Galbraith's warnings about Zia being heeded either in the White House or the State Department where the Pakistani president was seen as an invaluable ally and the key to the forthcoming destruction of the Soviet empire. Galbraith was, however, at least listened to by senators whose conscience was stirred by the treatment being meted out to the Bhutto women. They included both Pell and Senator Charles Percy, the influential Republican head of the Foreign Relations Committee.

It was Pell who famously cross-examined the then Under Secretary of State James Buckley, telling him, 'It appears as if President Zia is conducting a vendetta against the widow and daughter of executed—murdered—former Prime Minister Bhutto. I am wondering if the administration has made any representation to the government of Pakistan about the confinement and maltreatment of the Bhutto family.'

Galbraith himself recalls how he began campaigning for Benazir's freedom from 1981. As he told me shortly after her death:

> I was able to get people to write letters, or raise it with Pakistani Foreign Minister Sahibzada Yakub Khan who used to come to Washington all the time, and of course the Pakistani ambassador to the US.

Yakub loved being the urbane strategist and he couldn't defend the way she was being treated—he had this notion of himself as a chivalrous figure. I would get Pell and Percy to talk to him. At that time Percy had visited Pakistan a number of times, he'd been with Zulfikar Ali Bhutto when he'd changed from being president to prime minister. He always remembered that, always talked about that, and of course at that time Benazir was a young woman. In 1981 she wasn't even 30.

So these older senators had a kind of paternal interest in it and I was a young aide and they knew we were friends. People like that, like to help out staff. So that was the basic connection and I would talk to journalists and others.

The effect of Galbraith's campaigning became forcefully evident during Zia's December 1982 visit to Washington. Before he arrived one major irritant to the bilateral relationship was removed when the US Congress gave Islamabad a six-year exemption from the Symington Amendment prohibiting aid to any country involved in the illegal procurement of nuclear weapons' technology. By the time Zia touched down in Washington the Reagan administration had also cleared the way for a $3.2 billion military and economic aid package, including the sale of 40 advanced F-16 fighter-bombers to the Pakistan Air Force. One cloud remained in the form of Benazir. Her mother Nusrat had been allowed to leave Pakistan for medical treatment in November 1982, but Benazir remained a prisoner, refusing to cooperate with a military regime that promised her freedom only if she agreed to permanently forsake all political activity.

Shortly before Zia's arrival in Washington, *Time* magazine commented:

Zia's visit is a benchmark in Pakistan's relations with the US. Three years ago, rampaging demonstrators in Islamabad set fire to the US embassy, leading to the deaths of a US Marine, a US army warrant officer and two Pakistanis. In 1978 all US aid to Pakistan had been suspended because the Carter Administration believed that Pakistan was using US-supplied plutonium to develop a weapons-grade nuclear capability, an allegation Zia denies. But in 1981 Congress authorized a resumption of assistance, principally because Soviet troops had invaded Afghanistan.

Time's comment on Zia continued:

> Countless Pakistanis still hold him responsible for Bhutto's execution by hanging in 1979 after a show trial. Bhutto's Radcliffe-educated daughter Benazir, 29, remains under house arrest because her public appearance anywhere in Pakistan could instantly send thousands of her late father's supporters into the streets.

More interest in Benazir's fate was expressed during Zia's meeting with members of the Senate Foreign Relations Committee. Senator Pell was the first to ask about her, followed by a host of others.

'He talked about her inhumane treatment and this was not the atmosphere that Zia wanted,' Galbraith recalled.

> He got visibly upset and said, "Senator, you're very much misinformed. She lives in a nice house, better than any Senator's, she has use of the telephone, her friends can visit her." Immediately, I was there and went to use the telephone to try and call her. Of course she couldn't use the phone. But we decided to use the hook of the "friends could visit her" that now we could get permission to visit her. So we kept raising this.

If Zia's interaction with the Senate Foreign Relations Committee was a victory for Benazir's US supporters, there was more to celebrate in the months that followed. During Zia's December visit a number of senators wrote a letter to him expressing their concern about political prisoners in Pakistan, including Benazir. Zia took six months to reply. His formal and untruthful response the following June sent through diplomatic channels accepted that Benazir was under house detention to prevent her from engaging in political activities, but claimed she was 'given all comforts possible' and was allowed to meet with a wide range of friends and relatives. Galbraith contacted Benazir's cousins in Pakistan and established that she was ill with a severe ear infection, isolated, and far from comfortable. His findings were written up in a memo for Senator Pell who passed them on to Foreign Minister Khan when he next visited Washington.

Later in 1983, the Reagan administration nominated Deane Hinton as the next US ambassador to Pakistan. All US ambassadorial nominations have to be confirmed by the Senate, which can be a lengthy process involving a question and answer session before a Senate panel. In an unprecedented move at the time, senior State Department officials indicated they wanted Hinton to leave for Pakistan sooner rather than later, and if possible without the formality of a Senate hearing or confirmation session. Hinton had served in the US army during the Second World War and his biographical notes have him logged as a CIA employee from 1956, followed by a three-year stint with the State Department's Bureau of Intelligence and Research. It was just possible that the State Department wanted to avoid any lengthy and potentially embarrassing cross-examination about the new ambassador's intelligence connections before he assumed his new assignment.

A compromise was, therefore, agreed with key senators who met Hinton privately and told him they would back his departure for Islamabad without the formality of a hearing, provided he in turn used his position as ambassador to help facilitate a face-to-face meeting between Galbraith and Benazir. 'We made a deal with Hinton that we would let him go if he got me permission to see Benazir,' Galbraith later explained to me.

> That put the Pakistani government in the uncomfortable position that either I saw her when she was under arrest—and they obviously knew I would write about it and make a big deal about it—or they could let her go.

> The Reagan administration wasn't keen to help her at all. So the deal was, "you get to be the US ambassador and you use your weight to make them live up to their promise that I as a friend can visit her".

Hinton arrived in Pakistan in November 1983 to take up his ambassadorial position. The following month, late December 1983, the Senate Foreign Relations Committee asked Galbraith to visit South Asia, including Pakistan, to prepare a report on regional security issues.

Galbraith was scheduled to spend eight days in Pakistan in the first week of January 1984, deliberately keeping Karachi as his last stop in the hope that Zia would finally relent under American pressure and allow him to visit Benazir at home. He had in mind the deal that had been agreed with Hinton and was calculating what possible pressure the embassy could bring to bear on Zia. As he himself recorded at the time, 'This time the US Embassy was extremely helpful'. A decision on whether he could meet Benazir was imminent and would be taken by Zia himself. What actually happened was totally unexpected. Only hours after Galbraith flew into Karachi on 9 January 1984, Benazir was bundled on to a Swissair flight and left for Geneva. Galbraith's work took him to India for the next two days, but after that he flew to London for his first meeting with Benazir in years. 'I met her in London and we had lunch or tea at the Ritz,' he recalled.

> Then we walked around and that was a little awkward initially as we hadn't seen each other for six years. It was seven years since I'd seen her when she was president of the Oxford Union.
>
> It's awkward when you have someone whose been part of your circle and then touched by the kind of tragedy that she had—her father and imprisonment. It was something so alien and it was a little awkward and how do I respond to this? But she was very normal, she was herself, she was like the friend from Harvard. So then we discussed strategy and I said, "You need to come to the United States because basically the Reagan administration thinks you are a pro-Communist sympathizer against the US cause in Afghanistan, a radical, and they want to have this alliance with Pakistan. You need to be able to persuade them that you'll be just as good for them as Zia, except that you'll have more popular support."

Benazir took his advice and made her way to Washington within months of being released from Pakistan. Galbraith gave her the use of his personal apartment on Capitol Hill and took it upon himself to introduce her to as many senators and congressmen as he could. They included senators Pell and Percy, whom she met for the first time, Daniel Patrick Moynihan, John Glenn, Alan Cranston, and Paul Tsongas, as well as Congressmen Steve Solarz and Ben Gilman. Solarz was by all accounts captivated by her, but not very tactful when they sat down for lunch together at the House of Representatives. 'Have you read *Shame*,' he asked her, completely forgetting that she is 'Virgin Ironpants' who plays a starring role in Rushdie's famous novel.

Although the Reagan administration kept Benazir at arm's length for the duration of her March 1984 trip, she was given access to middle-ranking government officials, such as Assistant Secretary of State for Human Rights Dick Schifter and Geoffrey Kemp who had led the South Asia desk at the National Security Council. 'She's charming and beautiful and young and is able to say the right things to the senators,' Galbraith commented in retrospect. 'She does some media things and learns to talk slowly, making one or two points instead of being all over the place. She does it very well.'

It was the first major step of Benazir's climb to the top, and she had an old pal from Harvard and Oxford to thank for it. She returned to the US every year after that, improving her contacts with every visit. By the time of the Pakistani general elections of 1988, Benazir was one of the better known foreign politicians in the US, and she had some of the best contacts.

Galbraith's role in assisting Benazir was not restricted to advising her on how to improve contacts and win the confidence of US decision-makers. On election night in November 1988, he was once again at her side in Larkana, telling her how she should respond to the strong showing of the PPP. Zia had dissolved the National Assembly in May 1988 and called for fresh elections, just four days after the news leaked that a by now married Benazir was expecting her first child. PPP cynics immediately linked the timing of the elections to Benazir's approaching motherhood because, so they argued, a pregnant Benazir was seen as more vulnerable and less of a political challenge. The stakes rose higher still when Zia was killed. A caretaker government was in charge, sworn in by Acting President Ghulam Ishaq Khan, when the PPP with Benazir at its head emerged as the single largest party in the November 1988 elections.

Galbraith was among eight close family friends or relatives, including Nusrat and Zardari, who were gathered in the Bhutto's Larkana family home on election night. Outside the compound the world's press had gathered to record her reaction to the results as they started coming in. The PPP's strong showing had been predicted, but rather than focusing on the positive outcome of the election, Benazir's media team prepared a statement denouncing the authorities for permitting what they described as electoral fraud in specific constituencies that the PPP appeared to have lost.

'That's when I did the best thing for her entire career,' Galbraith explained.

> It's a very late night and her press people had prepared a statement denouncing the regime for electoral fraud, how the election had been stolen in Bahawalpur and Lahore and all those constituencies which the PPP should have won. She had enough sense to have some doubt about this and she showed it to me, asking, "What do you think?" I replied:

> "It's probably true, but I can promise you there's nobody in the world press whose heard of Bahawalpur and probably nobody in their audience. They're all here to cover the story of this beautiful young woman whose just been elected Prime Minister of Pakistan and the first woman to lead an Islamic country. Why don't you tell them you won?"

At that point Benazir had not been asked to form the government and her supporters were complaining that the election had been stolen. Galbraith's point was that she should not complain, but simply say she'd won without giving the authorities the choice of appointing someone else prime minister.

> And she said, "Will you write that?" So I wrote out a plain statement which she read. Something like, "The people have spoken, I am deeply honoured and my Party has the largest number of seats, twice as much as the next, and I expect the President will ask me to form the government. And it's with a great sense of responsibility and history and with the goal of improving the lives of the people of Pakistan ..."; that kind of thing.

> And then we left after dark, just after dusk and it was extraordinary. From the house in Larkana to Moenjodaro airport it was like 10 deep along the entire road. It about 20–30 kilometres.

> We got on the regular scheduled flight to Karachi. She had an exit row seat on one side and I on the other. It was a small propeller plane and the pilot came out and gave her three roses. We landed in Karachi and there were three million people at the airport. It was quite unbelievable. She had a Press conference there in some room they hadn't opened for 20 years.

> It was quite extraordinary and one of the most amazing days of my life to witness all that.

For the next two nail-biting weeks Benazir waited for the call that never seemed to come from the president's office inviting her, as the leader of the party that had won the largest number of seats, to form the next government. Benazir and fellow PPP members used the time to lobby foreign sympathizers to pressurize President Ghulam Ishaq Khan to give her the mandate she had earned. Individual letters pleading for support were hand-delivered to individual members of the US Congress and the British House of Commons.

In the final analysis however, it was all the effort she had invested in cultivating the US that finally paid off. At the end of November 1988, according to Galbraith, the new US ambassador to Pakistan, Bob Oakley, called on G.I. Khan at his presidential office, telling him, 'You have to choose Benazir, she's the leader of the party that got the most votes.' Khan listened; he had no choice. On 2 December 1988 Benazir took her oath as the first woman prime minister of the Muslim world.

Galbraith remained an invaluable friend, contact, and informal adviser of Benazir, especially as she prepared for her first state visit to the US as prime minister and the all important meeting with Reagan's successor, President George H.W. Bush.

In 1984 Galbraith had introduced her to fellow American lawyer, Mark Siegel, a former executive director of the National Democratic Committee and the Carter White House liaison with the US Jewish community. Siegel was so impressed by Benazir at their first meeting that he agreed to espouse her cause and become her unpaid lobbyist in Washington. As Galbraith became increasingly involved in the affairs of the Balkans—he was US ambassador to Croatia from 1993–98—the nitty gritty of consolidating Benazir's US contacts was left to Siegel. 'I worked happily for her pro bono until 1988, when she actually courageously hired me as her lobbyist, which was quite controversial in Pakistan,' Siegel confirmed to me. 'For a year I didn't have a name; I was known as Benazir's Jew.' Siegel remained her personal lobbyist even after she fell from power in 1996, went into self-imposed exile in 1999 after the Musharraf coup, and was no longer as welcome as she had previously been at the highest levels of the US administration.

Another turnaround in US attitudes began in early 2007 when Musharraf's personal popularity and credibility began to plummet in Pakistan. It became obvious to all concerned in the George H. W. Bush administration that it was only through Benazir that Pervez Musharraf could bolster his flagging political power.

Peter Galbraith had in the meanwhile remained ever more in the background during Benazir's first term in office. His own professional interests were taking him more and more to the Balkans, which meant less frequent contacts with Pakistan and the new prime minister. He remembered meeting her once when she came to Sarajevo as prime minister. There were occasional contacts too with other members of the family. In 1991, Galbraith's work as a senior adviser to the Senate Foreign Relations Committee took him to Damascus. Like me on an earlier occasion, he was staying at the local Sheraton Hotel where he recalled a dark- haired woman running up to him and throwing her arms around him. This was Sanam, Benazir's younger sister, and she was visiting Murtaza who was still based in Syria. As they approached the table where Murtaza was sitting, Galbraith was aware of his State Department escort melting away into the background. The reason was the collection of dubious foreigners, some from the Far East and some from Europe, who were sitting alongside Murtaza and his Syrian government minder.

It was a testament to their enduring friendship, however, that when Benazir's political enemies tried to smear her, they crafted a forged letter purportedly written by her to Galbraith urging him to use his influence to halt all military and economic aid to Pakistan. The letter addressed to Galbraith and distributed in September 1990, one month before she was dismissed from office, read:

> It would be most appropriate if military as well as economic assistance to Pakistan is stopped and all the International agencies like the World Bank, IMF are told to Squeeze the Government of Pakistan, and if possible all supply to Pakistan should be disrupted so that normal life in Pakistan comes to stand still.

The letter continued:

Dear Peter, Please use your influence on V.P. Singh the Indian Prime Minister, to engage the Pakistan army on the borders, so that they do not impede my way. I wish Rajiv Gandhi had been the Prime Minister of India, things would have been easier.

Thank you and with warm regards,

Sincerely yours,
Benazir Bhutto

6

THE INDIA LINK

IT WAS STRIKING HOW THE AUTHORS OF THE FORGED LETTER ATTEMPTED TO DISCREDIT BENAZIR BY portraying her as a traitor willing to sell out the national interest by conspiring with the US and India, the two foreign governments seen as key to Pakistan's future survival.

Relations with the US were ultra-sensitive. Although America had provided much of Islamabad's military hardware for the previous 40 years, and been the major source of foreign economic aid, any suggestion that a Pakistani ruler was prepared to get overly close to the US was bound to be viewed with suspicion on the Pakistani street. The link with Delhi was more complex. India had been Pakistan's traditional adversary from the time of Independence, and the two countries have engaged in three major wars in 1947–78, 1965, and 1971. Therefore, any notion of a Pakistani prime minister seeking the aid of the enemy to sort out their domestic problems was bound to be controversial.

However, elected civilian prime ministers like Benazir also needed to be on at least moderately friendly talking terms with Delhi to avoid the kind of Indian military build-up along the border that would provide the Pakistan army with an excuse to strengthen its grip at home. Achieving the right balance is a difficult and sensitive exercise. Standing aloof from India invited the risk of allowing an unchecked flare-up of tensions to develop into something more serious. Being too obviously friendly with India risked being cast in the perjorative mould of an Indian or Hindu 'agent'. Where India was concerned, it could be argued the dice was loaded against her long before she became prime minister. To begin with, her ancestry was against her. Islamic extremists in Pakistan never stopped taunting her with slighting references to her grandmother, Zulfikar's mother, Hindu-born Lakhibai who became Lady Khurshid after she converted, and her grand uncles who remained Hindu and stayed behind in India after Partition.

It was because of Lakhibai that Zulfikar's Islamic credentials were questioned until the day he died. The generals in charge of Pakistan in 1979, and who ordered Zulfikar's genitals to be photographed after his body was brought down from the scaffold, had convinced themselves that he was a bogus Muslim who remained true to his mother's original faith. The generals were also responsible for the scurrilous rumour that Lakhibai was in reality a courtesan who was never formally married to Sir Shahnawaz. Before moving in with Sir Shahnawaz she was alleged to have been the devoted partner of Motilal Nehru and the real mother of his only son, Jawaharlal, the first prime minister of independent India. By this reckoning, Zulfikar and Jawaharlal, to whom he bore a passing resemblance, were half brothers.

It did not help that Jawaharlal's daughter, Indira Gandhi, ostensibly Pakistan's and the Bhutto family's foe, was one of the first international leaders to make repeated pleas for clemency after he was sentenced to hang. Even US President Jimmy Carter did not weigh in on Zulfikar's behalf until much later. It was the same Indira Gandhi, then in opposition, who twice received Benazir's brothers, Murtaza and Shahnawaz, at her Delhi residence following their father's execution.

It was during that first meeting with Indira Gandhi in 1979 that

Murtaza suggested dividing Pakistan into four parts as a way of permanently blocking a future role for the generals. His controversial proposal for the dismemberment of Pakistan is recorded by his erstwhile colleague, Raja Anwar, in his book entitled *The Terrorist Prince*. Some Indian sources claim that the Bhutto boys asked for and were given generous funds at Indira Gandhi's behest, and those very sources hold that Benazir neither sought nor received any money.

Benazir's first personal exposure to the politics and conflicts that kept Pakistan and India at each other's throats came during the 1965 India–Pakistan war. She and her sister Sanam were at boarding school in Murree, close to the Kashmir border, when war broke out and the nuns in charge of the school made the girls participate in air-raid practices and blackouts. Six years later, as a college undergraduate at Harvard, Benazir was more directly involved when war broke out again, this time over the emerging nation of Bangladesh, and she was summoned by her father to New York to help him as he prepared his brief for the United Nations Security Council. It was while she was managing the telephones at her father's New York hotel suite and simultaneously acting as hostess for the delegations calling on him that Zulfikar gave Benazir her first lesson in international diplomacy.

When peace talks with India began the following year in the hill resort of S[h]imla, Benazir was once again at her father's side. This time she was personally introduced to Indira Gandhi and other Indian dignitaries, but it was her experiences at the mass level that made the greater impression. Her autobiography and other contemporary accounts record the ecstatic reception she received whenever she ventured out into the streets of S[h]imla, with traffic-jams and small mobs of enthusiastic Indians craning their necks to get a better view of her. One local newspaper carried the iconic headline, 'Benazir is benazir', roughly translating as 'The incomparable is incomparable'.

Many years later, when Benazir was prime minister of Pakistan in her own right, she hosted a visit to Islamabad by Indira Gandhi's son, Prime Minister Rajiv Gandhi. The occasion was a regional summit of

South Asian countries, and Benazir used it to try and forge a better personal rapport with Rajiv and his wife, Sonia, who were invited to a private dinner with Benazir and her husband during the course of the three-day visit. Six months later Rajiv was back in Islamabad, this time on a purely bilateral visit. The two visits led to a series of mutual confidence-building measures, including force reductions along the borders and an agreement that India and Pakistan would not attack each other's nuclear installations. Benazir would also claim many years later, shortly before she died, that she choked off assistance to militant Indian Sikhs who had been afforded refuge in Pakistan by General Zia. It was the termination of this support, she implied, that finished off militant Sikh demands for an independent homeland carved out of India's Punjab state.

Benazir's Indian critics charge her with being two-faced when it came to India. They compare her covert fostering of the Taliban under Major General Nasirullah Babar, later her interior minister, with her rallying cry to anti-Indian jihadi militants across both sides of the ceasefire line when she shouted 'Azadi, azadi ...' (freedom, freedom ...). Evidence that she was secretly and violently anti-Indian has been deduced from her television images of 1990 where she was seen inciting Kashmiri militants to take action against India's then governor of Kashmir, Jagmohan. Still remembered is the shocking cutting gesture she made at that time in 1990, her right hand striking the open palm of her left, as she intoned, 'Jag, jag, mo-mo, han-han'.

In her speech aimed at stoking the fury of the jihadists, she said:

The people of Kashmir do not fear death because they are Muslims. The Kashmiris have the blood of the mujahids and ghazis. The Kashmiris have the blood of mujahideens because Kashmiris are the heirs of Prophet Mohammed, Hazrat Ali, and Hazrat Omar.

And the brave women of Kashmir? they know how to fight and also to live. And when they live, they do so with dignity. From every village only one voice will emerge: freedom; from every school only one voice will emerge: freedom; every child will shout, "freedom, freedom, freedom".

French journalist François Gautier sensed the same hard line emanating from Benazir when he interviewed her in 1993 and asked her about Kashmir. She responded by telling him, 'You have to understand the Pakistani point of view on Kashmir ... that for long the Hindu Pandits in Kashmir exploited and dominated the Muslims who are getting back at them today.' Asked whether that was the only reason Pakistan was helping Kashmiris in their fight for self-determination, she replied, 'It should be clear also that Pakistan never forgot the humiliating loss of Bangladesh at the hands of India,' before adding, 'Zia did one right thing. He started the whole policy of proxy war by supporting the separatist movements in Punjab and Kashmir as a way of getting back at India.'

Benazir never attempted to justify her jihadi speech or the cutting gesture, but shortly before she was assassinated she claimed credit for reining in the Sikh extremists who had been given sanctuary across the border within Pakistan before she became prime minister.

Benazir's Sikh connection was revealed in December 2007 after India's National Security Adviser M.K. Narayanan publicly questioned her track record as 'not necessarily something which will make us believe that she would follow to the letter what she has said—I think even if she wishes to'. A furious Benazir lashed back in an interview with India's *Outlook* magazine:

> Does anyone remember that it was I who kept my promise to Prime Minister Rajiv Gandhi when we met and he appealed to me for help in tackling the Sikhs? Has India forgotten December 1988? Have they forgotten the results of that meeting and how I helped curb the Sikh militancy?

> If anyone kept their word, it was me. Not Rajiv. He went back to India and then called me on his way to the Commonwealth to say he could not keep his promise to withdraw from Siachen [the disputed glacier in northern Kashmir] and that he would do it only after the elections.

I had heard of Benazir's 'azadi' speech, as well as some of her other reported virulent comments about India–Pakistan relations, and wanted to see for myself just how much she had changed from the time we first met at Oxford. An occasion to talk to her freely and in depth arose when she invited me to visit her in Dubai in 2003. We had spoken over the telephone a few months earlier, and before that also briefly met in London. It was then that she and I agreed to get together for a heart-to-heart, somewhere private and away from the glare of television cameras.

One of the first questions I put to her before we sat down for dinner in Dubai was about Kashmir; how did she see Kashmir and was it a subject for negotiation? 'It's for negotiation and when I was prime minister, the Indian government had agreed to put Kashmir as an independent agenda item,' Benazir replied:

> We had two agenda items. One of the agenda items was Kashmir and the second agenda item was India–Pak and we said we must not let lack of progress on one issue impede progress on the other issue. The second thing … is that if we disagree over the territorial unity of Kashmir, we can still work for the social unity of Kashmir by working for safe and open borders. Because if we have safe and open borders, then people can travel, they can trade and then, ultimately, I feel we must ask ourselves that with a population of over a billion people and high rates of poverty amid islands of affluence, what do we do to pick ourselves out of this mess for the future? And I see the only way forward for us is to try and see what the European Union did and to try and have a kind of tariff in a common market that will enable people.

This sounded to me like sensible reasoning, at the very least sharply different from the kinds of sentiment associated with the *'azadi, goli chalao'* politician of a decade earlier. This new look, or rather a return to the old Benazir, had enhanced her reputation for expressing views that projected her both as sober and positive when it came to India. I in fact sensed something fundamental had changed. Speaking to her that day it seemed to me that Benazir had come round to the view that a nuclear armed Pakistan, one of the world's seven nuclear weapons powers, and India could no longer risk head-on confrontations. As she explained, 'After India and Pakistan went nuclear in 1998, PPP had a reappraisal and we said we don't want to follow tit for tat with India. Just because India does something, we should not copy it. We should identify our core interests and follow our core interests, but not copy India.'

Many in India still do not appreciate the importance of this changed thinking. In effect, Benazir had come around to the same point of view as the United States and Soviet Union in their time after they had tested nuclear weapons following the end of the Second World War. Both Moscow and Washington realized then that their nuclear arsenals ruled out any direct, face to face military engagements for the forseeable future. Hence the Cold War and the proxy conflicts that the two sides fought in theatres like Korea, Vietnam, and Afghanistan.

Benazir felt that what made sense for India and Pakistan was to strengthen economic ties. 'You know what makes economies move?' she asked me rhetorically:

> In my view economies move through the service sector, through creativity. So if we open up people will come and visit Pakistan, our hotels will be full, more hotels will be built, more labour will get jobs. Same in your country. All the visitors who come will want to have kebab and *tikka* and *nihari* and all the shops that make all the kebab and *tikka* and *nihari* will go up. People will want to buy, they will want to spend, they will want to go to museums, they will want to sight-see. It's the flow of money that strengthens our economy and that's what we all need—Nepal or Bangladesh or Sri Lanka or India, or Pakistan, we all need that.

Encouraged by what I had heard thus far, I focused more sharply on bilateral relations, asking Benazir if the bitterness among some Pakistanis was associated with their fear of Indians trying to reclaim the properties they had abandoned at the time of Partition. 'There is the older generation; they fear that, but I don't think there is any such thing among the younger generation,' she replied.

> I have met people who are very bitter about India and I am sure you have similar people on your side who have witnessed massacres. There was one particular lawyer I remember in Lahore whose father was massacred in front of him and he barely escaped with his own life. People who witnessed massacres, it's very difficult for them to let go.

> But, generally speaking, those who did not witness massacres, they

all want to talk about their homes in India which they left—and even Indians do the same. I met [former prime minister] Mr I.K. Gujral and he told me he had been in Jhelum his whole life. I have met [former deputy prime minister) Mr Advani and he told me about Karachi and Hyderabad.

It's all about diversity, America is about diversity, Britain is about diversity; it's all about unity through diversity.

I pressed on to ask if Pakistanis looked at Indians in a specific way. Did Pakistanis dislike Indians as such, anyone who held an Indian passport, or was it just the Hindus who were most intensely disliked?

'Well it changes from times of tension to times of less tension,' Benazir explained.

When there is tension and troops at the borders, then people hate anyone who is Indian, irrespective of whether they are Muslim or Hindu. They say, "They want to attack us and kill us, they want to destroy us and our country."

But when there is no tension, people really welcome Indians. I mean Indian films are very popular in Pakistan. Indian goods are smuggled across Pakistan all the time, people are desperate to get Indian visas and travel to India to go and visit their families, and go and see the Taj Mahal and the Mughal heritage of those days. And overseas, in America, I must have travelled to all the states where the Indians and Pakistanis and Bangladeshis see themselves as South Asians. They feel their interests are the same. They work together, they socialize together, there is no hatred at all.

You leave it to the people and they all want to be friends. Sometimes I think that your country and my country, our militaries need a war so that they can go on buying weapons. I don't know. But as far as the people level is concerned, there is a lot of love and affection.

I deliberately kept my most provocative question to the last, and when I put it to Benazir, she almost choked over the cup of tea in her hand. Looking her straight in the face I asked, 'As a Pakistani did you ever wake up in the morning and think, "Oh God I wish I could nuke a few thousand Indians?"'

Benazir's response was unequivocal:

For God's sake, never for a moment have I woken up with such a thought—because I know that nuking any Indian—if I was mad enough to think that—would end up nuking my own people. And this is sometimes what I don't understand because neither India can use the nuke, nor can Pakistan. Because whatever country is throwing that nuke knows there is not enough time space [to avoid retaliation] and is going to get it back. No.

7

THE NUCLEAR GAME

AMONG THE SUNDRY SECRETS THAT BENAZIR HAS TAKEN TO HER GRAVE ARE THE ORIGINS OF PAKISTAN'S NUCLEAR programme, her father's contribution to its success, and the role played by Pakistan's rogue nuclear scientists in exporting their deadly technology to countries like Libya, North Korea, and Iran.

In September 2003 I met a demoralized and unhappy Benazir in Dubai. Her husband was in prison back home in Pakistan, their children were growing up as expatriates, her mother had been claimed by Alzheimer's, she herself was in exile, and the military regime in Islamabad seemed too well entrenched to ever consider a return to democracy. In those bleak days, apparently bereft of any hope, a despairing Benazir told me in confidence of the part she played in sharing Pakistan's uranium enrichment expertise with North Korea in exchange for Pyongyang's missile know-how. One of the instigators of that exchange was A.Q. Khan, then the undisputed head of the Pakistani nuclear effort, including its all-important uranium enrichment facility. Years later Khan's role was authenticated by President Pervez Musharraf who documented in his autobiography,

In the Line of Fire (2006), how the renegade scientist had passed on to the North Koreans some two dozen prototype centrifuges for their enrichment experiments.

When I caught up with her six months later in March 2004 in London I asked whether she would be willing to talk on the record about Pakistan's nuclear ambitions, past and present. Six months on, however, she was much more confident in her own situation and her story had changed substantially. No repeat now of the references to overcoats and deep pockets for carrying secret CDs to Pyongyang. The most she was prepared to allude to was her symbolic role which only involved paying the North Koreans cash for their missiles. The clandestine export of Pakistan's nuclear data had indeed been all over the headlines just a few weeks earlier that year following A.Q. Khan's televised admission of guilt confirming that he had personally authorized the sale of nuclear exports to certain select countries. In his mea culpa broadcast over Pakistan state television from Islamabad, A.Q. Khan sought his countrymen's forgiveness for 'errors of judgement related to unauthorized proliferation activities'. He went on to say:

> I have much to answer for. The recent investigations were ordered with the government of Pakistan consequent to the disturbing disclosures and evidence by some countries to international agencies relating to alleged proliferation activities by certain Pakistanis and foreigners over the last two decades.
>
> The investigations have established that many of the reported activities did occur and these were inevitably initiated at my behest.
>
> In my interviews with the concerned government officials I was confronted with the evidence and findings and I have voluntarily admitted that much of it is true and accurate.

The roots of the proliferation mentioned by A.Q. Khan, and for that matter the genesis of Pakistan's nuclear weapons' development, are intertwined and go back three decades when Zulfikar was prime minister. At the time Pakistan had a modest nuclear programme built around a small Canadian-supplied nuclear power reactor, the Karachi

Nuclear Power Plant, abbreviated to Kanupp. Across the border, Indian scientists playing catch-up with China were far ahead of the game, and when, after the 1971 India–Pakistan war, an Indian general said he would soon have another 'present' for the Pakistani people, Zulfikar assumed he meant the development of an Indian nuclear bomb.

In 1972, top Pakistani scientists, with Zulfikar's backing and encouragement, held a series of meetings in Multan to discuss ways of upgrading their nuclear research to facilitate a bomb capability. These meetings assumed an added significance after the Indian test in 1974, prompting Zulfikar to comment that 'Pakistan would develop a bomb even if we have to eat grass'. It echoed an earlier statement when he said, 'if India builds the bomb, we will eat grass or leaves, even go hungry, but we will get one of our own. We have no other choice.'

Until 1974, as far as the outside world could gauge, Pakistan's intended route to the bomb lay through plutonium by illegally reprocessing spent fuel from the Canadian-supplied Kanupp reactor. The other route was through uranium enrichment, in which Pakistani scientists had very little experience and which was substantially more expensive. However, after the Indian test in 1974 everything changed. The Canadians tightened up their agreement with Pakistan and France began having second thoughts about supplying Pakistan with a reprocessing plant. This was where A.Q. Khan entered the picture. Four months after the Indian test, Khan wrote to Zulfikar offering his services to bring the bomb to Pakistan. At the time he was employed by the Physical Dynamics Research Laboratory (FDO) in Amsterdam, a sub-contractor to a three-nation consortium, uniting Britain, Germany, and Holland, working on new methods of uranium centrifuge enrichment. Khan's work for FDO gave him priceless access to the secrets of the new enrichment technology, as well as the worldwide range of contractors who supplied the consortium with the components required for the infrastructure. As long ago as 1980 a Dutch government report, entitled *Onderzoek zaak-Khan* concluded 'that it is likely that Pakistan through Khan has been able to acquire sensitive knowledge concerning the enrichment technology'. Subsequently, a Dutch court sentenced A.Q. Khan to four years imprisonment in absentia and the Dutch government declared him persona non grata.

Notwithstanding his criminal record abroad, Khan returned home to live the charmed life of a hero in Pakistan. The engineering laboratories he founded near Rawalpindi were re-named the Khan Research Laboratories (KRL) and his VIP status was further enhanced when Pakistan carried out a successful series of nuclear tests in 1998. His Pakistani supporters likened him to Albert Einstein, but any such comparison could only be described as farcical or absurd. The Nobel Prize winning Einstein was an original thinker, a physicist by training, whose theory of relativity revealed him to be a genius. Khan's discipline is metallurgy, and fellow scientists say he has above average competence, but his international fame—notoriety would be a better word—rests on his role in filching the secrets of the uranium-enrichment process from Holland and replicating it back home in Pakistan with the aid of an international blackmarket of suppliers he helped to create.

All this and more I related to Benazir one afternoon in 2004 as we sat in her London flat. She was all agog to hear everything I knew from a non-Pakistani perspective. I, therefore, also told her that what tipped the balance against Khan five years after the 1998 nuclear tests was the decision by Libya's Colonel Muammar Qadhafy to spill the beans about how his country had benefitted from Khan's nuclear experience. Why Qadhafy came clean is another story, but, assisted by his intelligence experts, the CIA came to the startling conclusion that Khan had amassed a personal fortune estimated at US$100 million through a global network of front companies prepared to supply nuclear know-how to anyone prepared to pay for it. Some of the other benefits in kind he is alleged to have acquired included a villa on the Caspian, courtesy of Iran, and a small share in the international sale of Iranian caviar.

For years arguments raged within the CIA about the merits of launching a covert operation to disrupt Khan's activities. Those who argued against such a move said it would endanger intelligence sources within Khan's empire. Eventually, the decision was made for the

Americans by Qadhafy himself when he went public with his decision to forswear all weapons of mass destruction. The knock-on effect from this declaration resulted in Khan's own televised admission of guilt and subsequent house arrest for leaking secrets. Even so, the full story of Khan's global network was never revealed in public, leaving unanswered the many questions and deep concerns of those seeking to halt the spread of nuclear weapons' technology.

Benazir knew the answer to at least one of those questions concerning North Korea but she wasn't talking, and I as her confidante from a few months earlier was sworn to secrecy. A later CIA report observed that Iran's nuclear programme received significant assistance from Khan. Officials pointed to the similarity of what Khan gave to Libya and Iran, asking why the Iranian deal should be any different from the Pakistani/Khan arrangements with Libya. One American expert, Gary Samore, who had served on the US National Security Council in the Clinton administration, revealed to me in private:

> The US wasn't aware that A.Q. Khan was in the nuclear export business until the very end of the Clinton administration when the CIA developed a new source of information providing insight into A.Q. Khan's activities in Libya.

> Through that same information the US also began to learn about A.Q. Khan's transfers, including to Iran and North Korea. It is clear, and in fact the Iranians have acknowledged this to the IAEA, that they received extensive assistance in the area of centrifuges [from Pakistan], but whether they also received nuclear weapons design from Khan is just not clear at this point.

Benazir listened patiently to my lengthy discourse, interrupting once to ask a question and at another time to confirm she had met Khan several times. Did he have a huge ego, I inquired? She smiled.

> The huge ego only started in 1980. When I knew him he was a modest man. I first came across him when he came to see me with Munir [Munir Ahmed Khan, the then chairman of the Pakistan Atomic Energy Commission]. They seemed like government servants ready to carry out government orders. The prime minister called them, they came.

Then Benazir looked at me and said she had heard some tittle-tattle about how I had crossed swords with Khan and she wanted to know the details. Taking a deep breath, I told Benazir about a newspaper scoop in which I had participated in 1979. In those days I was working for the *Observer* of London, and with a colleague, Colin Smith, I co-authored an exposé of Khan, entitled 'How Dr Khan Stole the Bomb for Islam'. Khan's furious response came six months later in a signed, handwritten letter, replete with 'Babu' English, and sent to the newspaper's editor. 'The article on Pakistan in the issue of 9.12.1979 written by Colin Smith and Shyam Bhatia was so vulgar and low that I considered it an insult to reflect on it,' Khan wrote.

> Shyam Bhatia, a Hindu bastard, could not write anything objective about Pakistan. Both insinuated as if Holland is an atomic bomb manufacturing factory where, instead of cheese balls, you could pick up 'triggering mechanisms'. Have you thought for a moment about the meaning of this word?
>
> Of course not, because you could not differentiate between the mouth and the back hole of a donkey. I do not owe an explanation to anybody, but I did owe an explanation to the Dutch government which I did with all the documents.
>
> Unfortunately, the followers of Jesus Christ are so honest and so nice and so upright in their professions that one must not say a word against it. All that the two journalists wanted was a cheap sensational article. Why don't you write about Margaret?
>
> You were quick to publish that article based on lies and concocted facts. *Impact International* has published an article on the BBC's vulgarity. For good journalism and to bring the public the other view, you should reproduce in the same way as you did with Smith and Bhatia.

A few years later he was back on the attack, this time focusing purely on me for another article I had written for the *Observer* in March 1987: 'I am sorry to note that a paper of such standing has allowed and is still allowing an Indian Hindu journalist, viz Shyam Bhatia, to use it as a propaganda platform against Pakistan and my person.'

Benazir raised her eyebrows and said nothing. I pressed on, asking,

'Khan never said anything to you like "Prime Minister, we must teach these wicked Hindus a lesson?"' She answered, 'Never. He was quiet; only spoke when questioned.' I persisted, 'But he is obviously completely crazy, a Pakistani Dr Strangelove, and obviously communal; and this is the man you all chose to revere as the Father of Pakistan's nuclear bomb.' Quick as a flash Benazir responded with a mini-explosion of her own, 'But he isn't the father of our bomb; we were ready to detonate the first nuclear device in December 1977.' She added that Pakistan had many other competent scientists, specifically listing Sultan Bashiruddin Mahmood, a Manchester, England-educated nuclear engineer who is considered by many to be the real architect of the Pakistani bomb. She also named and praised the former PAEC (Pakistan Atomic Energy Commission) chairman, Munir Ahmed Khan, a reactor engineer who trained at the Argonne National Laboratories in Illinois, saying he had been consistently undervalued as both a human being and a scientist.

Much of what Benazir went on to tell me that afternoon has never previously been disclosed, and was based on information exclusively provided to her by her father before he died. He was convinced that Zia would hang him and carry out a nuclear test at the same time to divert international attention from the execution. Benazir was 24 years old, a Harvard and Oxford graduate, when the army assumed power, toppling her father's government in a coup d'état. Both before and after the coup, she was privy to some of his innermost thoughts and secrets, including details of the nuclear programme. The world at large knows that Pakistan carried out six nuclear tests in May 1998 at its Baluchistan test site in response to five nuclear explosions conducted by India a few weeks earlier. Therefore, Benazir's assertion that Pakistan was ready to test two decades earlier in December 1977—six months after the coup—contradicts prevailing views and information about how far advanced along the nuclear path Pakistan was at that time.

'It was Munir Ahmed Khan who became chairman of the PAEC and my father who put together the team of scientists for this and he followed two paths to nuclear status,' she elaborated.

One was the reprocessing plant and he negotiated an agreement with France for a reprocessing plant, and then he did a uranium enrichment plant.

Now because the agreement with France was an open agreement, people focused on that and they were unaware that along with that there was a parallel effort. I don't think he necessarily kept it a secret, but nobody paid it attention because they jumped to the conclusion that the path we were following was plutonium and reprocessing. But we were following two paths, not just one.

After '77 my father told me that we were ready to detonate the first nuclear device, which we were making through the parallel programme—enrichment—in December 1977.

When I asked what happened to the December test project, Benazir replied, 'That was scuttled by Zia ul Haq, or maybe that just died on its own. I don't know. But there was a bomb that was ready for detonation in 1977. My father told me, I know it, I know it, A.Q. must know it, I know Ghulam Ishaq Khan must know it.'

Asked whether her memory was playing tricks, Benazir said:

No, I know my memory isn't playing tricks. We thought that Zia wants to kill my father, then detonate … I don't want to go into details for reasons of state. What my father thought was, Zia wants to kill him and, after killing him, he's going to go and detonate the device because Zia cancelled the reprocessing plant agreement.

So my father thought he's cancelled the reprocessing plant, but that's not the only way. We actually have the uranium way.

So he [my father] would always send back messages ... and I would be trying to contact Munir to find out where we stood. That, is it being detonated because it was December 1977? So first my father thought he will want to tie in things with his assassination [and distract attention], but apparently Zia decided not to detonate it.

According to Benazir, her father had set up a secret committee of top civil servants, including Munir Ahmed Khan, to authorize the purchase of vital components required for the test. Other members of the committee were Ghulam Ishaq Khan, then the finance secretary, State

Bank Governor A.G.M. Qazi and Foreign Secretary Agha Hilaly. It was this committee that authorized the purchase of vital spare parts for the nuclear programme.

Asked to be more specific about the spare parts, Benazir said, 'For buying the ... to put the parts together for the bomb. The components had to be put together. You had to set up the laboratory, you had to set up everything.' When asked to elaborate, she added:

> I don't know who else was working with Munir, I only know about Munir because I was trying to contact Munir throughout this time and briefing my father on what Munir had to say. Of course he would tell us, "Now it's on schedule, now it's been postponed to next year. Now it's been postponed to the year after."

Puzzled experts trying to make sense of what Benazir disclosed that afternoon agree that Pakistan in 1977 had neither the fissile material (plutonium or enriched uranium), nor the warhead design to test a bomb. Some speculate that, as China gave its nuclear warhead designs to Pakistan, the overall package may have included a Beijing-supplied rudimentary nuclear device for testing that was postponed for political reasons. Other US-based experts, who have asked not to be named, point out that the Chinese warhead designs were not passed on to Pakistan until the mid-1980s. One commented:

> The Chinese assistance happened much later. I don't think any of this makes much sense in terms of timing. In 1977 Pakistan did not have any reprocessing; there was only a small reprocessing facility at Pinstech. There was a pilot enrichment plant at Kahuta and a lab-testing facility at Sihala.
>
> It's possible that they got their material from some place else, or that Munir was telling Bhutto they were further along than they were. The last possibility is that she was talking of a cold test and that the PAEC had decided to carry out a test in laboratory conditions without using fissionable material.

The possibility of Munir exaggerating Pakistan's capabilities has been ruled out by Zulfikar's former press aide, Khalid Hasan. 'I knew Munir very well,' he told me in a telephone conversation from Washington DC where he is based as a journalist for a Pakistani newspaper. 'He was extremely cautious. He would not have advised for an explosion—the world would have pounced on Pakistan.'

When she became prime minister for the first time in 1988, Benazir had the opportunity to find out for herself what had happened to the December project. However, as she put it, 'They [the military establishment] tried to keep me out of the nuclear programme.' Her strategy was to ask for nuclear information from the army chief, he in turn referred her to the president. When Benazir asked President Ghulam Ishaq Khan where and when she could get a nuclear briefing, he told her abruptly, 'There's no need for you to know.' That was when she retaliated by making direct contact with some of the key scientists, including Munir and A.Q. Khan. 'I could sack the scientists and then what would they [the army] do?' Benazir asked rhetorically.

> Or I could take the press into confidence, I could take parliament into confidence. So then, because I asserted myself, the president called me up within hours of my calling the scientists and telling them I wanted a briefing.

> He [the president] said, "Come, we'll have a meeting together." So then we decided to set up a command committee. Originally, the programme was under the prime minister who was the chief executive. When Zia took over as president, he kept himself as the head of it because under Zia the chief executive was the president. So it went to the president and the army chief.

> When I became prime minister, they tried to keep it with the president and the army chief, but later they inducted me and it became the president, the prime minister, and the army chief. We would meet at the presidency and when we wanted briefings on anything, we would call the scientists.

Benazir insisted she was not in favour of testing Pakistan's nuclear weapons, partly as she did not want to engage in a tit-for-tat exercise with India and also because, as she put it, 'How many bombs do we need to destroy civilization?' Her solution was to authorize a series of cold tests without using stockpiled fissile material. The cold tests were carried out during her first term of office between January and March 1989, but they did not satisfy the army or the scientists. One Pakistani source, Karachi-based journalist Syed Saleem Shahzad, claims that the first cold test was actually conducted in 1982. Shahzad told me early in 2008 that he had no documented evidence to back up his assertion, explaining that his information was based on a conversation he had with an unnamed scientist.

Just prior to her dismissal from office in 1990, Benazir discovered that her political commitment not to produce weapons-grade uranium (beyond 60 per cent and more) had been breached. Her source of information was American Ambassador Robert Oakley, who told her how US satellites had picked up the information by monitoring the speed at which the enrichment plant at Kahuta was working. It was the equivalent of non-intrusive inspection because, in Benazir's own words, 'The satellites could pick up the speed at which the enrichment plant was working ... with these revolutions—because at 60 per cent you beat at a certain level and at 90 per cent you beat at another level.' The weapons-grade enrichment continued between the time of her leaving office in 1990 and her return to power in 1993.

Once back in office in 1993, Benazir asked why the original commitment had been breached. She was told that some of the nuclear cores in storage had deteriorated, and in order to replenish them the scientists had bypassed the political guidelines by exceeding the 60 per cent enrichment levels privately and previously agreed with the Americans. To ensure future compliance with government policy, Benazir said she instituted a system of security within the Kahuta enrichment plant. This was to monitor the scientists, she explained.

It was a no-win situation for the prime minister. The scientists had the backing of the army and the ISI, and were determined not to be held back. The more she tried to enforce a policy of nuclear restraint, Benazir explained, the greater were the number of conspiracies hatched to bring her down. One of the thriller-style conspiracies involved elements from the ISI and military intelligence concocting a plan to abduct A.Q. Khan, so that political responsibility for failing to ensure his safety would fall on Benazir and prompt the early dismissal of her second government.

> Those elements were basically the intelligence of the ISI people and MI [military intelligence] ...They were trying to overthrow my government, but these people had some journalists very close to them. One of them planned to take A.Q. Khan to a Muslim country and keep him there.

> They told him [Khan] they would take him on a pilgrimage ... and keep him there. I saw this as an attempt to embarrass me by suggesting that Benazir is anti-Pakistan and she's a security threat and she's responsible for the disappearance of our nuclear scientist. So I passed orders that no scientist could leave the country without government permission.

These orders instituted by Benazir's government are of historic importance because they make a mockery of Musharraf's later claims that the many visits made by Khan, 19 in the course of a single year according to one estimate, to countries such as Iran and Libya, as well as to southern Africa and the Gulf, were all undertaken at his personal initiative and without prior government knowledge or permission. Benazir, for her part, was insistent that she did not condone or approve of nuclear exports, although, given what she had told me the previous year about her role in the North Korean deal, this was at best a partial truth.

Key military officers, and Khan himself, are believed to have made huge financial gains from exporting nuclear hardware. Benazir acknowledged hearing stories of that kind but defended Khan, saying he had not made as much money from nuclear sales as some people claimed. 'I think Khan got a pittance of the money. He couldn't even leave the country without somebody on his left hand and right hand watching everything he did.' Benazir said that her own and only inadvertent role in facilitating contacts with the international blackmarket for nuclear items went back to 1989–90 when impoverished Soviet scientists approached her through third parties with an offer to sell highly enriched uranium.

> There were Soviet scientists who were starving ... they were poor, their salaries had inflated or something or the other and they wanted to meet me and I didn't want to meet them.

They approached the government, parliamentarians, anybody who could give access to the prime minister. Please remember this is a time when the newspapers are all writing about the nuclear issue and we all think our nuclear programme is under threat ... so here they come and say, "Well we don't have to worry if we can't make uranium, we can buy uranium, okay?"

I thought that it was a trap the intelligence had set up ... so I sent them [the Soviet scientists] to the ISI to investigate; unfortunately, if it was not a trap, I introduced the ISI to the network.

Asked about Pakistani nuclear exports to Iran, Benazir told me:

My suspicion is that Iran happened ... between 1990 to 1993. The reason I have this suspicion is because a certain conversation took place which I don't want to get into. And I said we would not export to Iran even if we had a military understanding with them.

Libya comes much later, when I was overthrown a second time. Either they offered it to them then or maybe they offered it in my first term, I don't know. But in February 2000 Musharraf went to Libya. In July, Musharraf's commerce minister and friend took out a full page ad offering nuclear products for sale.

When inquired which commerce minister she was referring to, Benazir replied, 'Abdul Razak, the Adamajee boy—Razak [the scion of one of Pakistan's richest families].' Benazir said secret Pakistani nuclear sales transactions conveyed the impression that all the country's nuclear assets were up for grabs, just so long as the price was right:

To give the impression that our nuclear assets are so vulnerable as to permit infiltration and solo actions by single scientists makes it seem as though the state is incompetent and it cannot be trusted with its nuclear assets.

My concern is that there will be a terrible backlash and everyone in Pakistan, including myself, would like to see our nuclear secrets safeguarded. We would like to continue to be accepted as a nuclear state. I fear that we cannot do so unless we come clean on this issue and that we work with the international community to put in safeguards so we can keep our nuclear assets and we can give confidence to the world community.

8

DEALING WITH THE GENERALS

T HE WAY BENAZIR WAS COLD-SHOULDERED BY HER ARMY
CHIEF IN 1989 WHEN SHE ASKED FOR A BRIEFING ON
nuclear issues was symptomatic of a wider problem of trust between the
military establishment and the Bhutto family. Indeed, with a few singular
exceptions, most of the army top brass, who routinely siphoned off 35
per cent of the national budget for military expenses, resented the
'common touch' popularity of both Zulfikar and Benazir. They saw
both father and daughter as a threat to their own dominant role in
Pakistani politics.

Among the few exceptions was General Tikka Khan, the 'Butcher of
Bangladesh', who was Pakistan's chief of army staff from 1972 to 1976.
A veteran of the British Indian army who saw action on the Burmese
and Italian fronts, he opted for Pakistan in 1947, and by all accounts
distinguished himself in the 1965 India–Pakistan war when he
successfully defended the city of Sialkot from Indian attack. His more
controversial years came later in 1971 when he was sent to then East
Pakistan as governor and chief martial law administrator. His brutal
crackdown on East Pakistani civilians, code-named Operation

Searchlight, included members of the Awami League headed by Sheikh Mujibur Rahman, and earned him a reputation as a brutal and ruthless military officer. Both Pakistan's military ruler at the time, General Yahya Khan and Zulfikar saw him in a different light. Yahya appointed him chief of army staff and Zulfikar, who considered him a safe pair of hands, appointed him as his defence minister. Benazir never forgot how he remained loyal to her father, even taking on the role of PPP secretary general when the party was in turmoil after Zulfikar's execution. When Benazir came to power for the first time, she appointed him governor of Punjab, an assignment he held for two years until her government fell. In talking about him to me Benazir always described him as a 'fine person'. When he died in 2002, Benazir commended him as a person who 'rose to the highest offices of this country due to his hard work and respect for the rule of law'.

It was Benazir's personal misfortune that another army general and Tikka Khan's immediate succesor, Zia ul Haq, orchestrated the judicial murder of her father. He was not her father's first choice, she told me, and indeed superseded half a dozen others. He had however a proven record of loyalty to the civilian government and there were no blemishes on his record associated with alcohol, women, or the misuse of state funds. Thirty years later another army general, Pervez Musharraf, also ostensibly without blemishes, was in charge of the country when she was assassinated in Rawalpindi. The hostility that Benazir aroused among many of the generals who ran the Pakistan army also extended to key officers in charge of the military intelligence agencies, MI (military intelligence) and ISI (inter services intelligence). They included ISI chief General Hamid Gul who was sacked by Benazir in 1989 and replaced by General Shamsur Rahman Kallu following speculation that the ISI and MI were jointly planning a coup to unseat her. Shortly after he was fired, Gul remarked contemptuously of Benazir that she was a prime minister who hadn't even understood the difference between the country's intelligence agencies.

Yet even after Gul's departure, the ISI remained hostile to Benazir and the PPP. The ISI's anti-Benazir bias was highlighted in the run-up to the September–October 1989 no-confidence motion in the National Assembly, when two senior ISI officers launched Operation Midnight Jackal. Benazir was provided with tape-recordings of this eventually unsuccessful operation to bribe or intimidate members of the National Assembly to vote against her PPP government.

The army has dominated Pakistan's political life ever since Independence in 1947. The process started under Sandhurst graduate Major General Iskander Mirza, the country's last governor general and first president, who was overthrown in 1958 by his army chief, General Ayub Khan, who was in turn succeeded by General Yahya Khan. After the brief interlude of Zulfikar Ali Bhutto, a different army chief, this time General Zia ul Haq, ruled Pakistan for a further 11 years. Zia's death brought Pakistan back to civilian rule, although the army retained a vital backstage role until General Pervez Musharraf overthrew the elected government of Prime Minister Nawaz Sharif in 1999.

Benazir loyalists hold that out of the six army commanders with whom she has had to deal, Zia included, only three could be considered decent, loyal, and worthy of the prime minister's trust. They were Asif Nawaz, chief of staff from 1991–92, Abdul Wahid Kakar from 1992–94, and Jehangir Karamat, later ambassador in Washington DC, who was army chief between 1996 and 1998. Each has been portrayed as a constitutionalist because they believed in strengthening and nurturing Pakistan's democratic institutions. Now, however, the habit of meddling in politics is so deeply ingrained that even the finest officers find it difficult to remain detached. This includes the saintly General Kakar who turned down an extension. It was he who mediated in 1992 between President Ghulam Ishaq Khan and Prime Minister Nawaz Sharif. Following his intervention both men resigned.

When Benazir returned to power in 1993, she asked Kakar to stay on, but to his credit he said he had had enough and wanted to retire. She had reasonable relations too with General Karamat. He was seen as an able professional committed to democracy. After Benazir was dismissed by her own civilian-appointed president, Farooq Leghari, Karamat did not interfere.

Benazir at Greenville, Mississippi: Benazir attended college in the United States from 1969–73.

Harbouring ambitions of her own: Benazir at the S[h]imla Summit in India in 1972, with Foreign Affairs Minister Swaran Singh, where she accompanied her father Zulfikar Ali Bhutto, then prime minister of Pakistan.

▲ A charismatic personality: Benazir took active interest in politics even during her Harvard and Oxford days.

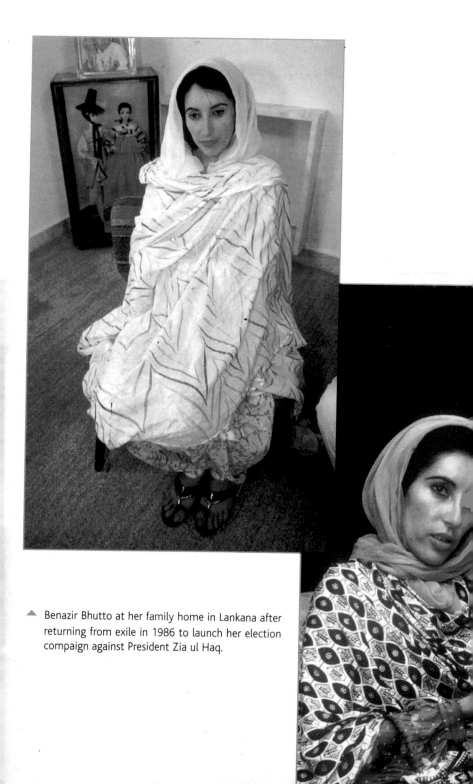

Benazir Bhutto at her family home in Lankana after returning from exile in 1986 to launch her election compaign against President Zia ul Haq.

Benazir sitting in front of family portraits of her father Zulfikar, mother Nusrat and brother Murtaza.

On her wedding day, Benazir with her mother
Nusrat (left), sister Nasim (right) and husband
Asif Ali Zardari.

▲ Benazir being sworn in as prime minister
on 19 October 1993 by interim President
Wasim Sajjad.

Benazir with her children: (L-R) Aseefa, Bilawal and Bakhtawar. (Photo courtesy: Shyam Bhatia)

Heir apparent: Benazir with her son Bilawal. (Photo courtesy: Shyam Bhatia)

On a state visit to the US in 1989: Benazir Bhutto with George H. W. Bush.

Benazir with Nawaz Sharif at a joint press conference on 3 December 2007 in Islamabad.

Benazir reads from the party mainfesto at her last compaign rally in Rawalpindi on 27 December 2007.

Mourning the loss of an outstanding leader: Supporters of PPP hold a candlelight vigil for Benazir Bhutto at Bilawal House in Lahore.

<u>Pakistan Peoples Party</u>

To the officials and members of Pakistan Peoples Party I say that I was honoured to lead you. No leader could be as proud of their party, their dedication, devotion and discipline to the mission of Quaid e Awam Zulfikar Ali Bhutto for a Federal Democratic and Egalitarian Pakistan as I have been proud of you. I salute your courage and your sense of honour. I salute you for standing by your sister through two military dictatorships.

I fear for the future of Pakistan. Please continue the fight against extremism, dictatorship, poverty and ignorance.

I would like my husband Asif Ali Zardari to lead you in this interim period until you and he decide what is best. I say this because he is a man of courage and honour. He spent 11½ years in prison without bending despite torture. He has the political stature to keep our party united.

I wish all of you success in fulfilling the manifesto of our party and in serving the downtrodden, discriminated and oppressed people of Pakistan. Dedicate yourselves to freeing them from poverty and backwardness as you have done in the past.

Benazir Bhutto
October 16, 2007

Benazir's one page handwritten will.
(Photo courtesy: Shyam Bhatia)

Just before he died, Zulfikar wrote with contempt of the military dictators who step into the shoes of elected civilian governments:

> Tin-pot dictators have ravaged Asia, Latin America, and Africa. They are the worst tyrants of the post-colonial period. They have destroyed time-honoured institutions and treated their people like animals. They have caused internal divisions and external confusions. The dictator is the one animal who needs to be caged. He betrays his profession and his constitution. He betrays the people and destroys human values. He destroys culture. He binds the youth and makes the structure collapse. He rules by fluke and freak. He is the upstart who is devoid of ideals and ideology. Not a single one of them has made a moment's contribution to history.

The military for its part was just as distrustful of Zulfikar and treated him accordingly. Zia repeatedly branded him a traitor, telling army colleagues that he was actually a Hindu (a huge insult for some paranoid Pakistanis) masquerading as a Muslim. His taunt was a deliberate dig at Zulfikar's immediate ancestry, for as we have noted, his mother, Lady Khursheed Begum, was born a Hindu called Lakhibai who converted to Islam when she married Zulfikar's father, Sir Shahnawaz Bhutto. On the other hand, Lady Khursheed's brothers retained their faith and migrated to India after the partition of the subcontinent.

Both Murtaza and Benazir told me separately how it was under army instructions that their father was badly treated and tortured beyond endurance before he was taken to scaffold in April 1979. Benazir once told me, with tears streaming down her face, how she was given a detailed account of the treatment meted out to Zulfikar's body after he was brought down from the scaffold. (This was different from Murtaza's version to me, which was that his father was dead before he was hanged.) Sympathetic but horrified army contacts told Benazir how his body was stripped of its loose trousers or *shalwar* and a photographer was told to photograph his genitals to see if he had been properly circumcised according to Islamic custom. 'No dignity permitted, not even in death,' was Benazir's comment to me.

This description of how her dead father was treated was later confirmed by the army officer present at the hanging, Colonel Rafi Uddin, who said in his Urdu language book, *Bhutto's Last 323 Days*:

> A photographer, who had been sent by an intelligence agency, took some photographs of Mr Bhutto's private parts because the authorities wanted to confirm if he had been circumcised in the Islamic manner. After the photographs were taken, it was confirmed that he was circumcised in the Islamic way.

In Benazir's eyes, 'Cobra Eyes' Zia was the worst of all the generals. He was the Jalandhar, India-born officer who overthrew the PPP government in 1977, arrested her father, and then had him sentenced to death after packing the bench with judges willing to take orders from him. 'It's either him or me,' Zia was widely reported as saying just before Zulfikar was hanged for a crime that he went to his death protesting he did not commit. After the hanging, Zia is said to have told fellow officers, 'The bastard is dead.'

Both before and after her father's death, Benazir and her mother were repeatedly arrested, released, and then re-arrested. In March 1981, following the birth of the Movement for the Restoration of Democracy, she was arrested yet again and sentenced to five months solitary confinement. A further two years of detention followed in virtual isolation until she was allowed to go abroad on medical grounds in January 1984.

General Aslam Beg, who succeeded Zia, was outwardly civil, but demonstrated his disrespect for Benazir in subtle ways. It was Benazir as prime minister who observed that he was always bareheaded when she visited him at army headquarters, not realizing at the time that in army tradition a bareheaded officer without his peaked cap is not required to salute his superiors.

Although not as obsequious as Zia, General Pervez Musharraf was the image of the smartly turned out and 'correct' officer when he first met Benazir. Her image of the army had been inevitably coloured by her sole experience of meeting Zia in 1977, when he bowed and scraped and told her what an honour it was to meet the daughter of such a great man. Three months later the 'great man' was under arrest and Zia had taken his place. Benazir's initial meeting with Musharraf took place early on in her first term of office. She was hosting a visiting Turkish delegation and Musharraf, who had served at the Pakistani diplomatic mission in Ankara, was her official translator. In those days he held the rank of brigadier, and Benazir described him to me as 'very bright and smart'. She didn't remember him as a whisky drinker (he is said to enjoy a daily tipple) or a dog lover, but said he was quite a 'jolly officer'. Others in the PPP described him as 'slimy' and the general who preferred to use his stiletto rather than a broadsword to deal with opponents.

Benazir believed that relations between them soured over what is widely known as the Kargil plot approved by General Aslam Beg and supported by the then ISI chief General Hamid Gul. The plan was to infiltrate Pakistani-financed mujahiddin across the Kashmir ceasefire line in Kargil, and start a war with India ending with the Pakistani conquest of the Kashmiri capital, Srinagar.

The Beg–Gul plan had many supporters, including Pervez Musharraf, among the top brass of the Pakistan army. Musharraf's job was to argue its merits in front of Benazir. She remembered being quite disappointed by what she heard. 'I was quite disappointed in his analytical skills,' she recalled.

> He was my director general military operations and he presented me a plan in front of 50 officers about how the mujahiddin would infiltrate an area similar to Kargil and how they would bring about a war. The Indians wouldn't be able to dislocate us and so they would be forced to fight a second front by attacking Pakistan—at which point the international community would intervene and we'd take Srinagar.
>
> I said, "General, they'll tell me take your troops back." But I think he personally doesn't like me because of that confrontation that he and I had in GHQ on the Kargil issue. But believe me I had to have that confrontation because if I did not ... the blood of 3,000 soldiers would be on our hands. I did not allow it, but after I was overthrown they went ahead with the Kargil folly and 3,000 of our young boys, our officers and men, the best in our army, died. So many on the Indian side died; there was so much bitterness. The whole world had to intervene to stop it escalating into a potentially nuclear war.

So I'm told he personally doesn't like me for that reason, although other people tell me he's very personable. He once spoke to me and said he has nothing against me.

Whether or not he had anything 'against' her, Musharraf kept Benazir at arm's length after he overthrew the elected government of Nawaz Sharif and packed the deposed prime minister off into exile in Saudi Arabia. As the new best friend of the West in the fight against Islamic terrorism, Musharraf had ample financial and political support from abroad. Events played into his hands in 2003 when Geneva magistrate Daniel Devaud convicted Benazir and her husband in absentia. The charge was money-laundering. Now Musharraf could also present himself as the champion of the underdog in the fight against corruption. A year earlier he had felt sufficiently strong to play a cat and mouse game with the PPP, which had emerged as the single largest opposition party in the 2002 general election.

Musharraf's wily plan was to divide and rule by offering the prime minister's job to Benazir's deputy, PPP Vice President Makdoom Fahim, who was within an ace of accepting until Benazir told him his first job after taking the oath of office would be to announce a general amnesty for all political exiles. Fearful of upsetting either the general, or Benazir, or both, Fahim turned down the job. Wajid Shamsul Hasan, Pakistan's former high commissioner in London, was asked by Benazir to advise Fahim. He subsequently told friends how Fahim was informed that the key issue was the amnesty, and that if Musharraf genuinely wanted a reconciliation with Benazir and other members of the opposition, he would approve. Fahim proved reluctant and Musharraf's offer to appoint him prime minister was withdrawn.

The cat and mouse games with Benazir would have continued indefinitely, but Musharraf's own vulnerability was exposed after a series of attempts against his own life after 2002. The fight against the terrorists was also going nowhere when he made his critical error in 2007 by clamping down on Pakistani lawyers and judges. They included Chief Justice Iftikhar Chaudhry who was removed from his position and placed under house arrest, the first time this had happened to a Pakistani chief justice.

The resulting unrest and repeated questions about Musharraf's suitability and legitimacy created a new window of opportunity for Benazir who was rediscovered by the West as the champion of Pakistani democracy and a future political partner for Musharraf, rather than as a beleaguered politician defending herself against corruption. Equally suddenly, Benazir's responses to questions about Musharraf were unexpectedly muted. Party loyalists were disappointed by her toned-down backing for the arrested chief justice and were unimpressed by what her inner circle defended as important 'tacit support' for Chaudhry. One of Benazir's senior advisers at the time explained her tactics, saying, 'She didn't go overboard, but she was supporting him; she issued [a] statement demanding his release and reinstatement; all these things were done by her. It was PPP workers who were first attacked and killed in July.' We need to have smooth transition to democracy through free and fair elections,' Benazir told me by way of justification in October 2007.

> We need a government in place that has the mandate of the people. Towards this end the steps taken include first a promise by General Musharraf to the Supreme Court of Pakistan to retire as army chief; second, establishment of a parliamentary ethics committee; third, recognition of the role of the opposition in a political system; fourth, steps towards a transparent vote count; and, fifth, acknowledgement and termination of a political vendetta. Of course there is much more to be done in terms of holding fair elections, but this is a start.

She did have second thoughts about Mussarraf after he declared a state of emergency in November 2007, cracking down on judges, journalists, and politicians after it became evident that the Supreme Court was likely to rule against his eligibility for re-election as president. Outwitted and apparently out-manoeuvred by the man with whom she had agreed a power-sharing deal only a few months earlier, Benazir for a long time refused to condemn him in strong terms but her supporters insisted that she be allowed to keep her options open.

It was in my last interview with her towards the end of 2007 that I asked whether she could share her latest impressions about Musharraf following their meeting of reconciliation in Abu Dhabi. I wanted to hear what new words she would use to characterize the man she previously described to me as a 'maverick' and 'military dictator' who had taken his country down the path of ruination. I was awaiting an answer when, in a message from Pakistan, Benazir's answer popped up on my computer screen: 'I know you are curious,' Benazir told me, 'but you will have to wait for another time.'

9

THE YEARS IN POWER

B ENAZIR HAD BEEN MARRIED FOR JUST OVER A YEAR AND
WAS THE MOTHER OF A THREE-MONTH OLD BABY BOY
when she was sworn in as prime minister of Pakistan on 2 December
1988. She would go on to enjoy two terms of office. First between 1988
and 1990, a total of 20 months, and then again for three years between
1993 and 1996. Critics who describe her time in office as deeply flawed
and unproductive are especially scornful of the first period when they
say her government failed to pass a single major piece of legislation. The
reality was far more complex. From the day she was sworn in, Benazir
faced a hostile Troika of the new army chief, General Aslam Beg, the
acting president, Ghulam Ishaq Khan, and the intelligence services in the
form of Military Intelligence (MI) and Inter Services Intelligence (ISI)
under General Hamid Gul, who refused to cooperate with her
government and were determined to break her.

In Pakistani politics the country's power-sharing Troika was
traditionally made up of the president, the army chief, and the prime
minister. But, in Benazir's time the prime minister was excluded from the
Troika which now consisted of the president, the army chief, and the

head of the ISI. This new Troika's all too obvious contempt for her gender and her Bhutto family heritage coalesced in a political straitjacket they created, within which they tried to contain Benazir long before she emerged triumphant in the 1988 elections.

As prime minister, Benazir committed some errors of judgement. These included her personal role in conveying nuclear weapons technology to North Korea in exchange for Pyongyang's nuclear secrets. Another misjudgement was to pander to the jihadist Kashmir lobby with her near hysterical cries of 'freedom, freedom'. A third was her reluctance to challenge the ISI strategy of building up the Taliban as the future government of Afghanistan. However, while they cannot be ignored, these misjudgements mentioned in earlier chapters need to be seen in the context of a beleaguered prime minister fighting for her life against the entrenched forces of a right wing military establishment and its allies. Small wonder then that Benazir was unable to pass a single major piece of legislation during her first 20 months in office. She had other more important issues to deal with closer to home, and survival was at the top of her list.

It was Zia ul Haq who allowed Benazir to return home in 1986, but when the old dictator was assassinated new options materialized for Pakistan in general and Benazir in particular. Before he died, Zia had scheduled elections for November 1988, and the immediate choice before the Troika was whether to permit the planned elections to go ahead, or to use Zia's death as an excuse for re-imposing martial law. Their decision to permit the elections to be held as scheduled was conditional on the exercise being held with individuals standing without any formal party affiliations. This was the tactic Zia had used a few years earlier to prevent the PPP from asserting itself as a rival political force in parliament. Members of the Troika also took comfort from the fact of Benazir's pregnancy. She was expecting her first child only weeks before the election date and was not expected to be as fully engaged as she otherwise might have been.

Two subsequent developments had an immediate effect on the political landscape. Bilawal, Benazir's first child, was born a month early, in September, freeing up his mother for last minute campaigning. The following month, in a shock decision, the Supreme Court ruled in response to an appeal from the PPP that political parties would be allowed to participate in the elections because party-less elections violated the fundamental rights guaranteed by the Constitution.

The Troika's immediate response to the court's decision was to back the formation of a coalition of political parties opposed to the PPP. This new coalition, alleged to be generously funded by the ISI, with funds provided by Gul, was known as the Islami Jamhoori Itihad or IJI. A politically astute General Beg ensured that all his options were covered by sending Benazir a message offering his personal commitment to holding free and fair elections on schedule, but asking in return that he be confirmed as army chief if she won. He was responding to speculation that the acting president wanted to ease him out of his job by appointing him to the more ceremonial position of chairman of the joint chiefs of staff committee. Benazir told me years later how she sent Beg a written message giving him the pre-election commitment he sought from her.

On 16 November 1988, despite blatant vote-rigging by the ISI, the PPP emerged from the polls as the single largest party in parliament, winning 93 seats against the IJI's 54. A similar pattern emerged in the provincial assembly elections that followed, with the PPP's impressive showing in all four provinces of Punjab, Baluchistan, North-West Frontier Province (NWFP), and Sindh. It was only in Sindh, however, that the party gained an outright majority. Efforts to prevent Benazir from forming the next government continued until the last possible minute. Close family friends and allies, like Wajid Shamsul Hasan, who would be appointed high commissioner to London during Benazir's second government, recalls the frantic and unsuccessful attempts to persuade newly elected PPP legislators to switch to the IJI. The prime minister's position was even dangled in front of Benazir's mother, Nusrat, if she could form a coalition without her daughter's participation.

The public mood was clearly behind Benazir. So much was evident in the huge rallies she had attracted in the days and weeks preceding election day. As Khan nervously consulted the Troika and other representatives of Pakistan's military–bureaucracy combine, American Ambassador Robert Oakley stepped in with a personal intervention in Benazir's favour. Three weeks after the election a self-evidently reluctant G.I. Khan finally contacted Benazir and invited her to form the next government.

An exasperated Benazir would tell friends at social gatherings months after the event how a reluctant acting president ensured that she was the last to be called upon to form a government, and that only after the Troika had failed to bribe, cajole, or browbeat a sufficient number of PPP legislators to cross the floor. Failure to break the PPP and achieve a workable deal with some other party leader, such as Zia's protégé Nawaz Sharif, left Khan with no alternative to Benazir.

'They tried to make a deal with everybody under the sun,' she told her biographer Muhammed Ali Sheikh. None of them had the number. 'We had the magic number and they were unable to make a deal. And when they were unable to make a deal, I was invited.' The Troika's unrelenting hostility meant there would be no let-up in the feud with the new prime minister. As far as Benazir was concerned, a vindictive hate campaign and deliberate slights continued unabated from the day she was sworn in. Minutes after she was sworn in, Khan forced out a few obligatory words of congratulations before announcing that he was leaving for the mosque to participate in his daily Islamic routine of prayers. When Benazir asked if she could join him at the mosque, he replied it was for men only, before adding as an afterthought that she was free to watch if she so wished. Later that same day, in what Benazir saw as a bid to test her mettle, Khan told her that a hijacked Russian aircraft was headed in the direction of Pakistan. Whether the acting president expected his new prime minister to collapse in hysteria or tears, he did not say. The crisis was dealt with by one of Benazir senior aides who intervened to say that all the country's airfields would be blocked to prevent the hijackers from landing in Pakistan.

Khan's responses amounted to an early warning for Benazir that she would have to remain on her toes, no matter what, and she would have to battle for her voice to be heard on policy issues or when it came to making senior government appointments. As Benazir discovered to her cost, the outcome of these skirmishes was hard to predict and by no means guaranteed to go in her favour. The struggle over appointments began with the presidency. When Zia's plane crashed, Ghulam Ishaq Khan, as head of the Senate, was immediately sworn in as acting president. The Troika was in favour of his continuing. Benazir had her reservations. She had been put off by Khan's attitude shortly after she arrived for her first day of work at the prime minister's office. On that day, and for several days following, not a single file was brought to her for comment or a decision. When Benazir brought this to Khan's attention, his response was one of indifference. It was only when Benazir threatened to go public with her concerns that Khan ordered government civil servants to include the prime minister in the decision-making process by sending her relevant documents for discussion and approval.

Soon after the election, Beg made clear to the new prime minister that there were certain areas of government where the military would brook no interference from Benazir. Defence and, by extension, the key intelligence agencies, was one. Foreign affairs was another. Hence the decision to ask Zia's appointee, Sahibzada Yakub Khan, to stay on in the same job. In practical terms, this further confirmed the army's exclusive control over developing nuclear weapons' programme, Afghan policy, and freedom to collaborate at will with anti-Indian jihadists operating across the ceasefire line in Kashmir. There was an additional tussle over the finance minister's portfolio. The army was in favour of retaining the renowned economist and World Bank adviser Dr Mahbub ul Haq. Benazir had other candidates in mind. In the ensuing compromise she kept the finance portfolio and appointed a former State Bank governor, Wasim Jafri, as her financial adviser.

The same spirit of give and take was absent when it came to the president's job. G.I. Khan had been acting president for three months before the general election. Three months later, as preparations began galvanizing the electoral college for the presidential election—made up of the national parliament and four provincial assemblies—Beg asked Benazir if she had any particular candidate in mind. The appointment was a critical one because under the Zia-inherited constitution it was in the president's gift to appoint a new army chief, as well as to both appoint and dismiss the prime minister. Benazir's first choice was Malik Qasim, a veteran of the Movement for the Restoration of Democracy, who had dared to challenge Zia. He was unacceptable to the army. So too was retired General Tikka Khan, a former army chief, who threw in his lot with Zulfikar and was later secretary general of the PPP. In an effort to maintain peace with the Troika, Benazir reluctantly agreed to back Khan. It was a decision she would live to regret.

Soon after being sworn in, Benazir managed to obtain Khan's approval to change two of the four provincial governors. It was, however, a different matter when it came to a major military appointment later in 1989. It was Benazir's argument that year that the incumbent chairman of the joint chiefs of staff, Admiral Iftikhar Ahmed Sirohey, had reached retirement age and needed to be replaced. Khan argued that the appointment of such senior military officers was his exclusive prerogative and Sirohey would stay put for the next two years. In the end it was the president's wishes that prevailed. Similarly, it was Khan-supported candidates in 1989, backed by the Troika, who were separately confirmed as chief justice of the Supreme Court and chief election commissioner.

Khan and Beg had each won their separate trials of strength against Benazir. The same was true of the third member of the Troika, spy chief Hamid Gul, who took the initiative in early 1989 to undertake an extraordinary foreign adventure that ended in humiliation for Pakistan. As head of the well funded and all powerful ISI and a self-proclaimed Islamist, Gul had earned the praise of the Americans for organizing the mujahiddin resistance to the Soviet invasion of Afghanistan in 1979. Ten years later he came up with a brand new plan to cross the Afghan border and take control of the town of Jalalabad and surrounding areas. The ostensible reason for the operation was to create a provisional capital in Jalalabad from where the Islamist-dominated and anti-Soviet Afghan opposition could operate. The real reason, according to Benazir's aides, was Gul's belief that he could conquer Jalalabad by force and claim it in the name of Pakistan.

A ranking lieutenant general in the Pakistan army, Gul presented himself as a super patriot, authorizing the despatch of Pakistani troops for the Jalalabad operation in April 1989 where they were soundly thrashed and repulsed by the Afghan army's 11 Division. Gul tried unsuccessfully to blame Benazir, saying someone in the prime minister's entourage had leaked the details of his plan to the Afghan authorities. Several years later the whole sorry episode was recalled by Wajid Shamsul Hasan:

> I remember in 1989 Hamid Gul was ISI chief and he wanted to conquer the Afghan border town of Jalalabad and give it back to Pakistan as a gift. He organized an invasion by regular Pakistani troops ... but they had a very heavy beating by [Afghan President] Najibullah's soldiers. Najibullah presented himself as an Afghan nationalist and told his people that their motherland was being invaded by their neighbour. The Afghani troops and local people became very angry ... not least because there was a lot of arson and rape. So that mission failed with heavy casualties.

The botched Jalalabad exercise anticipated by almost a year another equally disastrous bid by the Pakistan army to wrest control of the strategic Kargil sector in Kashmir from India. Like Jalalabad, that too ended in disgrace, defeat, and retreat.

In the ensuing scandal over who was responsible for Jalalabad, Gul was moved sideways to take over as corps commander in Multan. Two years later he was Nawaz's choice to take over as army chief when Beg retired. However, as fortune or circumstances dictated at the time, he was overlooked. Following the Karachi bombings in October 2007, Benazir wrote to Musharraf naming Gul as one of those involved in the conspiracy against her. He was placed under house arrest on 4 November 2007 after Musharraf declared a state of emergency.

As the Gul fiasco played itself out, the simmering feud between

Benazir and Khan was compounded by the tensions between the prime minister and ex-president Zia's most ambitious protégé, Punjab Chief Minister Nawaz Sharif. In later years, after he himself had been removed from power by the army and forced into exile, Nawaz mended his fences with Benazir and praised her as his sister and partner in the struggle to restore democracy. In 1988 however he was her sworn enemy. During Zia's lifetime Nawaz was perceived by some Pakistanis as a potential long-term successor to the dictator. When Zia died so suddenly, Nawaz's own political hopes and expectations were thwarted by the loss of his all-important backer. He responded by strengthening his ties with the Troika and creating as many political difficulties as possible for Benazir.

Nawaz's idea of making life hell for Benazir was to regularly question the authority and remit of her federal government in his home province of Punjab where he ruled as chief minister. He did this first of all by refusing to observe the standard protocol of receiving her whenever she visited the Punjab. Ministers in his provincial cabinet were given licence to characterize her as a *kaffir* or infidel and an enemy of the state. Religious elders based in the Punjabi capital of Lahore delivered sermons on an agreed date in March 1989 questioning the Islamic credentials of a government headed by a woman prime minister. Benazir responded in an interview given to the American CBS network:

> Sovereignty belongs to God. Men and women are his trustees. The trustees vote for a government. Therefore, as the trustees have voted for government, that government has come into being by the will of Allah as the expression of His sovereignty. So it is Islamic to have a government led by a woman.

Another of his stratagems, begun in late 1988, was to ban contact between the Punjab local government agencies and their federal counterparts in Islamabad. When the federal government exercised its right to rotate civil servants assigned to the Punjab, Nawaz questioned Islamabad's motives and threatened to expel all Punjab-based federal civil servants. When the federal government asked Punjab to release civil rights advocates imprisoned under Zia's martial law regulations, Nawaz accused Islamabad of trying to ride roughshod over the rights, sensitivities and local autonomy exercised by Pakistan's provincial governments. He rejected out of hand Benazir's proposal that Islamabad and the Punjab should at least agree to a minimum joint agenda for tackling such key issues as the war on narcotics and illegal weapons, as well as tackling health, education, and cost of living concerns.

Ignoring Benazir's peace overtures, he focused his energies on building up a parliamentary opposition to threaten her power base in Islamabad. In April 1989, following a series of meetings with the Troika in Islamabad, Nawaz announced the creation of a new Combined Opposition Parliamentary Party (COPP), comprising his own IJI and a PPP breakaway group, National People's Party, headed by Ghulam Mustafa Jatoi. When Benazir was dismissed from office in August 1990, Jatoi, a fellow Sindhi, served as interim prime minister until fresh elections brought Nawaz to power.

Meanwhile COPP expanded its composition to include other members of the opposition, amending its title to the Combined Opposition Parliamentary Front (COPF) which moved the November 1989 no-confidence motion against the PPP. The no-confidence motion failed but not from want of effort by Nawaz. In the run up to the vote, his IJI party cadres rounded up some 60 opposition MPs and held them under lock and key at two hotels at Murree. On the day the no-confidence motion was tabled they were bussed to Islamabad to cast their votes.

Hemmed in by such individuals as Beg, Gul, Khan, and Nawaz, there was not much scope or indeed opportunity for Benazir to pursue her own ideas of political change. The seven-part, 42-section party manifesto she introduced before the election included her personal pledge to create a Pakistan free of exploitation, poverty, and injustice, and a country in which the party promised to meet every citizen's basic need for food, clothing, housing, education, and health. It was a populist manifesto echoing the past promises of Zulfikar that Benazir had no hope of implementing. She did not help her cause by appointing her mother as senior minister without portfolio and her father-in-law as chairman of the parliamentary public accounts committee. Both appointments may have been perfectly justified in Benazir's eyes, but they led to predictable accusations of nepotism. So did the creation of the Placement Bureau, which allowed the prime minister to make political appointments to senior civil service positions.

The impression of ineffectual governance overshadowed Benazir's very real and underestimated achievement in advancing the democratic process by releasing political prisoners and lifting media censorship, although even here her hands were tied. Shamsul Hasan was entrusted with the task of breaking up the National Press Trust, a conglomerate of over 15 newspapers that had been created by the previous military regime of General Ayub Khan as a means of controlling the press. It took Shamsul Hasan the best part of 18 months to draw up detailed proposals to disband the Trust. When he prepared a summary for Khan to sign in advance of parliamentary approval, the president sat on it, postponing his signature. It was still unsigned when the government fell in 1990, and it was only when Benazir returned to power in 1993 that the Trust was formally dissolved.

Unable to discharge her responsibilities, Benazir embarked on a series of foreign trips that saw her travel at dizzying intervals to all parts of the globe. One day she was in Beijing, then it was Tokyo, Manila, London, Ankara, Washington DC, New York, London again, Paris, and other world capitals. The trips enhanced her image as the first woman prime minister of an Islamic country, and in Kuala Lumpur in 1989 she at least had the satisfaction of personally shepherding Pakistan's re-entry into the Commonwealth. In practical terms, however, many of these extended foreign trips, regardless of the toe-curling praise received from party and family loyalists, were of questionable value.

When she threw her personal weight behind what appeared to be new directions in foreign policy, she succeeded only in alienating those she most wanted to impress. Earlier chapters have recorded in greater detail her 'azadi, azadi' calls over Kashmir that dissipated much of the goodwill she had generated in India following two lengthy sessions of talks with Rajiv Gandhi. Similarly, her role in facilitating the import of

North Korea's missile technology may have earned her praise from the Pakistani military establishment, but in the longer run it raised doubts among some of her otherwise loyal American supporters who wondered whether she could ever really be fully trusted.

Soaring inflation, high unemployment, and a growing drugs problem all added to Benazir's woes in 1989. Drug abuse became an especially shaming and worrying issue during her first term when Pakistan was established as a major exporter of heroin. Chronic abusers of heroin increased from 20,000 in 1980 to over 10 times that number a decade later. By 1993, the start of her second term, there were 3.01 million drug abusers in Pakistan, of whom over a million were heroin abusers.

What prompted a still deeper crisis for Benazir, precipitating the dismissal of her first government in 1990, was the escalating violence in her home province, Sindh. It began when the minority MQM party, representing the Muslims who had emigrated from India during and after 1947, called for a general strike in Karachi in 1990. As the strike escalated into violence, Benazir found she had to call on the army to restore law and order. By August 1990, with the violence in Sindh showing no signs of abating, G.I. Khan dismissed the federal government on grounds of corruption, inaction, and incompetence. A caretaker government headed by COPF leader Jatoi was installed until fresh elections later that year brought Nawaz to power.

There were fresh grounds for optimism for Benazir when she was re-elected prime minister for the second time in 1993. The power of the Troika was broken with Beg's retirement in 1992 and Khan's departure from office the following year. Nawaz's conflict with Khan in 1993 over who had greater authority led to another constitutional crisis and fresh elections in which the PPP once again emerged as the party with the single largest bloc of seats. Another issue that went in Benazir's favour was the election as president of PPP stalwart Farooq Leghari, which was greeted at the time as a triumph for democracy and national stability.

Yet, for all the positive post-election signs, the fight seemed to go out of Benazir during her second term. Whether it was the 1988-90 experience that soured her, or whether she lacked the mental stamina necessary to run the country, there was a sense of drift throughout her second term. For all the party propaganda about how she was a proven election winner, the question that repeatedly arose was whether Benazir was capable of ruling. One test of her grip on power was how the PPP government dealt with the Afghan Taliban. Originally a student-based Islamic resistance movement, the Taliban were created by the ISI with massive funding from the CIA to counter Soviet influence in Afghanistan. Declassified US intelligence documents reveal Washington's concerns in the early 1990s about Pakistan providing weapons, money, and fuel to help the Taliban gradually take over the whole of Afghanistan. Ironically, nearly 20 years later, the US and Britain spent their time and resources to kill the Taliban beast they had helped to create.

When Benazir was criticized in later years for her government's support of the Taliban—later revealed as the hosts of Al Qa'eda terrorists—her stock response was that the Taliban were creatures of the ISI over whom she had no control. A few weeks before she died, Benazir finally took some responsibility for the Taliban, saying, 'We all thought the Taliban would be a factor for peace, and we were wrong.' The earlier party line was however typified by the response of Major General Nasirullah Babar, one of Benazir's key aides, who complained about the ISI to the *New Yorker* magazine:

> We had no control over these people. They were like a government unto themselves. The ISI, the army, and the president had been running the show for so long that they simply didn't want to give it up. They got so carried away with the jihad that, unwittingly or not, they got involved with all these fundamentalist movements across the Islamic world. They thought that once they got Afghanistan they'd go across to the Soviet Central-Asian republics and into Kashmir.

An equally convincing argument was advanced to explain why Benazir was unable to advance her own pet project for the greater empowerment of women in Pakistan. In her many interviews with the foreign media during her second term, Benazir boasted of her successful initiative in appointing women judges, a women's division in the Pakistan government headed by a top level female civil servant, all-women police stations, and even a women's bank. Speaking after her own election victory she said, 'It means a lot not only to Pakistani women, but to women the world over. It has given women a role model and an example. And it also upheld something that many Muslims believe in: that men and women are equal in the eyes of God.' However, on the more substantive issue of repealing the fundamentalist laws inherited from the Zia years that curtailed women's rights, she had less to say. Women's groups had pointed out, for example, that under Zia Islamization laws, including the Hudood ordinances, the burden of proof in rape and adultery cases was weighted against innocent women victims. The least a woman prime minister was expected to do was rectify the balance. Benazir's cronies responded that her hands were tied because she lacked the necessary two-third's majority in parliament to legislate the required changes.

As the drift continued unchecked, Amnesty International published a damning report in January 1995, entitled *Pakistan: the Pattern Persists— Torture, Deaths in Custody, Disappearances and Extrajudicial Executions under the PPP Government.* Commenting that Benazir's government had not done enough in its first 15 months of office to safeguard human rights, the report called for the abolition of death sentences for prisoners of conscience and urged that the death penalty for children be abolished.

It was the bitter family feud dividing the Bhuttos that captured public attention and sapped so much of Benazir's energy during her second administration. The dispute that pitted mother against daughter and sister against brothers had its origins, according to one source, in the hundreds of millions of dollars paid to Pakistan by oil rich Arab rulers and the Shah of Iran during the last years of Zulfikar's life. Like the Shah, who is said to have given Pakistan US$500 million for the bomb it was developing, the Arabs also wanted a slice of Pakistan's nuclear cake. Foremost among them was Libya's ruler, Colonel Muammar Qadhafy, who asked Zulfikar if he could have the first bomb off the assembly line. Qadhafy's gung-ho interest is chronicled in *The Islamic Bomb* by Steve Weissman and Hebert Krosney published in 1982. The authors quote a former European Director of Pakistan International Airlines, the late Mohammed Beg, who told them that PIA special flights were used to physically transport some US$200 million in cash from Tripoli to Islamabad. Zulfikar, according to other sources, was distrustful of his closest associates and paid the Libyan money into his personal bank Swiss accounts.

How this money should be used and who should be responsible for its distribution were the reasons why, according to these sources, Nusrat and her children were regularly at daggers drawn. The other reason for the long running and unresolved family feud was power. When Murtaza eventually returned to Pakistan for good in 1993 and challenged his sister's leadership of the PPP, Nusrat helped him organize his election campaign for the Sindh provincial assembly where he contested some 23 constituencies to demonstrate that he was more popular than Benazir in their all-important family home province. In the event, he won only from a single constituency. Benazir was so infuriated by her mother's role in helping Murtaza that she outset her from her position as co-chair of the PPP. Her mother responded by saying of Benazir, 'I had no idea I had nourished a viper in my breast.'

Nusrat, who described Murtaza as a 'lovely boy', earlier took the lead in negotiating the terms for his return to Pakistan where he was wanted on terrorism charges. In 1993 Nusrat told US journalist Mary Anne Weaver:

> He wants to enter politics here, and people are now negotiating, on my behalf, with the army and the president, but he must be given an amnesty, and his return must be announced two weeks in advance. I don't want him to come back in secret through the back door. He must be received properly by the people of Pakistan. He is, after all, Zulfi Bhutto's son.

Weaver's interview with Nusrat, published in the *New Yorker*, also had Zulfikar's widow saying:

> I was to have been my husband's political heir. But, because I was ill, I told the party that I would like Benazir to stand in my stead. They couldn't

make her chairman, because I already was, so they coined the phrase "co-chairman", which we both still are.

The hostility that developed between mother and daughter was nothing compared to the enmity that mushroomed between Benazir and Murtaza, on the one hand, and Benazir and Zardari on the other. The expletives (deleted) that Murtaza used to describe his sister, when I interviewed him, were mild in comparison to the language he used when speaking to other members of the foreign media. In one unpublished interview with a visiting *New York Times* reporter, Murtaza even went so far as to say that if he had an opportunity to kill Benazir, he would. This bitterness dividing Benazir and Murtaza transcended the generations. Murtaza's daughter, Fatima, unequivocally blamed her aunt for her father's death. 'If she didn't sign the death warrant, then who had the power to cover it up? She did,' Fatima said in one much-quoted interview in 2007. In another pointed criticism of her aunt, Fatima commented in an op-ed piece for the *Los Angeles Times*:

> My father was a member of parliament and a vocal critic of his sister's politics. He was killed outside our home in 1996 in a carefully planned police assassination while she was prime minister. There were 70 to 100 policemen at the scene, all the streetlights had been shut off, and the roads were cordoned off. Six men were killed with my father. They were shot at point blank range, suffered multiple bullet wounds and were left to bleed on the streets.

She added:

> To this day, her role in his assassination has never been adequately answered, although the tribunal convened after his death under the leadership of three respected judges concluded that it could not have taken place without approval from a "much higher" political authority.

10

EXILE

ONE BRIGHT SUMMER MORNING IN DUBAI IN 2003, BENAZIR STOOD UP IN FRONT OF AN ASSEMBLED CROWD of family friends and party loyalists to present a 338 line poem that highlighted the pain of living in exile. The Harvard and Oxford graduate, and two-time prime minister, was dressed in her familiar green and white shalwar kameez, the colours of the Pakistan flag. A white dupatta or scarf covered her head and shoulders as befitted a respectable married woman from her country.

Invitees arrived in groups of four and five, negotiating their way past the empty pillbox guarding her front door, past her suspicious guard dog, Caesar, into the hall with the shelves carrying her collection of books on cookery, yoga, health, and astrology, past the giant-sized pictures of Zulfikar and Zardari, until they were ushered into the spacious front room of the pink villa generously made available to her by the United Arab Emirates government.

As flunkeys offered soft drinks, cups of green tea, chocolates, samosas and traditional South Asian sweets on expensive Harrods china, Benazir told her guests that the poem was inspired by the story of a legendary heroine from Sindh, Marvi of Malir, who resisted the gifts, jewels, and wedding proposal of a powerful local ruler in favour of a life of patriotism, chastity, and simplicity. The inferred parallel with her own personal situation was deliberate. She too was a persecuted woman from Sindh who would rather suffer rather than accept the bribes and enticements on offer from unjust local rulers.

In all the years I had known Benazir, she had never before shown any evidence of giving into the forces ranged against her. Yet the Dubai poem, which marks her fiftieth birthday, opens with a Koranic or Biblical reference to Adam and continues with 'I am nearer home than my heart's beat' contained unmistakeable traces of self-pity and was written in a whimsical, self-indulgent style that seemed somehow to be out of place for this former prime minister of Pakistan.

She would later tell friends that thoughts about her late father, dead brothers, and jailed husband were uppermost in her mind as she composed those lines. At times she seemed close to breaking down, prompting many in the carefully chosen audience, some of whom had specially flown in from Pakistan to mark the occasion, to reach for their handkerchiefs.

About her favourite younger brother, Shahnawaz, she wrote, 'Shah returned home whole his soul went free, No stranger to the soil, Embracing his body in death, Making it part of the legends of our land, When his last breath came, We carried him to the hidden coolness of the desert sand.' Her eulogy for Murtaza was half plea and half memorial, prompted by memories of their happier times together at Harvard and Oxford: 'God do not take the brother that I love, It was too late, he was gone, Again I buried a brother.'

By that sunny day in Dubai, Benazir had been living abroad in exile for four continuous years. Zardari remained locked up in a Karachi prison and there was no immediate prospect of either husband or wife regaining their political freedom back home in Pakistan. In that sense, therefore, the frustration that comes through in the lines of her poem was entirely consistent with the longing of an exile yearning for an opportunity to return home. 'Strands of white my hair now shows, my face is gaunt with sadness, I to my people want to go. O where is my husband gone,' she recited.

Critics described the poem as lacking any literary merit whatsoever, unkindly comparing it to a pre-election manifesto. In reality there was no way for Benazir to anticipate the date of the next free election in Pakistan, and the poem was much more an indication of her gloomy state of mind that year. Hence the themes of incarceration, injustice, and cruelty that reverberate through the lines that took some 45 minutes to recite. Supportive friends say on that June morning Benazir revealed herself as the feisty campaigner ready to fight injustice, as well as her family's and her own destiny to right perceived wrongs in Pakistan.

'My heart longs to fly with them,' she said in her clear voice reverbrating through the front room of the pink villa that had become her home away from home. 'Invisible chains hold me prisoner, the wounds of the past fester again for my country and me.' Afterwards, as she mingled among her guests, she related how her childhood experiences of living away from her parents had helped sustain her in later years. It began with the Catholic boarding school in Murree, to which she was sent as a 12 year old. Later at Harvard, where she spent her first term alone and weeping in her dormitory room, and subsequently at Oxford, she learnt to cope for herself. 'I learned to look after myself,' she would reveal in one of her many interviews with her Harvard contemporary Amy Willentz:

> I have lived a life of contrasts, and I give thanks to God that I was in the US in those hippie days and we were all so informal ... I could go to airports and pick up my own luggage and make my own bed. I came from so privileged a background; there I became self-sufficient. In the face of what later happened to me, I would have crumbled otherwise.

All this from a woman who had previously lived the life of some colonial princess, rarely cooking her own meals, or even walking to the post office because the family chauffeur was always on duty to transport her like some precious object to wherever she wished to go.

Fortunately for Benazir, she had in her brother Murtaza at least one familiar face she could count upon for some of the time at both their universities. He was younger and took up his place one year after her at Harvard, so they were not exact contemporaries. In the same way as she and Sanam found solace in each other's company at Murree, so she and Murtaza in those easier and happier times at both Harvard and Oxford each knew there was a shoulder to cry upon in times of stress.

When she first went into exile in 1984, following ceaseless harassment from Zia's agents and long periods of imprisonment, including solitary confinement, Benazir's first port of call was Geneva where her mother was undergoing treatment for cancer. It was there that she also met up after four and a half years with her Kabul-based brothers, before going on to establish an independent base for herself in London. That was more familiar English-speaking territory, close to the friends she had made at Oxford and the legions of PPP supporters who saw in her a future prime minister of their country. In those distant days, Benazir first rented a flat in the high-rise Barbican complex, close to St Paul's Cathedral, where her mother would also stay during her frequent visits from Geneva.

Once, after attending a PPP rally nearby, I ran into mother and daughter as they scurried back to their Barbican home. It was the first time I met Nusrat face to face. Benazir fidgeted with her scarf as she introduced us. Then they were gone. A year later I went into the flat for the first time to offer my condolences over Shahnawaz's mysterious death a few weeks earlier in Cannes. Benazir's face was swollen and her eyes were red from almost continual weeping. She was dressed all in black and sat on the carpeted floor with her feet drawn up under her. We did not speak, but she acknowledged my presence by nodding her head.

It was from the Barbican home that she made her triumphal return to Pakistan in 1986. When her first government was dismissed in August 1990, she and Zardari resolved they needed a more permanent London base which they could call their own. They bought an apartment in fashionable Queensgate, a short walk from Hyde Park, cheek by jowl with the house where Sanam had also set up home. It was to the Queensgate apartment that I was invited whenever Benazir happened to be visiting London, and where I was invited to share family meals and, on one occasion, even take family photographs of Benazir with her three children. The sheer convenience of the apartment's location was underlined years later when Benazir and Nawaz agreed to patch up their differences. Queensgate is only a 10 minute taxi ride from where Nawaz has his London home on the other side of Hyde Park, just off Park Lane. Benazir's erstwhile political rival started off his life in exile following the 1999 military coup by establishing himself in Saudi Arabia. A few years later he moved to London to be closer to his brother Shabaz and other overseas supporters of his Pakistan Muslim League (PML-N).

Nawaz was still in Jeddah when Benazir visited Saudi Arabia on pilgrimage early in 2006. She used the opportunity to call on him and offer her condolences for the loss of his father. It was a human gesture to which Nawaz responded by suggesting they find ways to end their long-simmering political feud. Matters were helped by Nawaz's imminent move to London and by the friendly intervention of Luis Ayala, secretary general of Socialist International. He told both Benazir and Nawaz that resolving their differences was an essential prerequisite for Pakistan's return to democrated government. When eventually the two finally decided to bury the hatchet after months of negotiations in 2006, it was relatively simple to arrange alternate meetings at each other's London homes.

A key role was played by the Cambridge-educated and Lahore-based lawyer, Aitzaz Ahsan, who had been Benazir's legal representative and a cabinet minister in her second government. Significantly, he had also been retained as legal counsel by Nawaz when the former prime minister was overthrown and imprisoned by Musharraf in 1999. Trusted by both sides, he was brought in to preside over a committee of four senators— Senators Raza Rabani and Safdar Abbasi from the PPP and Senators Ahsan Iqbal and Ishaq Dar from the Pakistan Muslim League (Nawaz)—to work out a joint agreed plan of action. 'Yes, the idea was to set up a working understanding with the other side,' Ahsan would later recall.

I came into it almost on the last day when I was asked to fly in from Lahore. They did want my input. I gave some kind of thoughts to the draft; it was a competent draft. I can't claim the complete, total authorship of the draft, or that I made it more cut and dry, but both considered my input as necessary, there's no doubt about that.

Nawaz also requested my presence because, although basically I was PPP and her associate and I'd been leader of the opposition in Nawaz Sharif's prime ministership—and I'd been a very rigorous critic—he also sort of trusted me. In fact he retained me as his lawyer when he was Musharraf's prisoner.

The rapprochement was a huge achievement by any standards. Nawaz had been a protégé of Zia, the man who hanged Zulfikar, and the PPP liked to paint him as a sidekick of the military and Pakistan's ultra-religious establishment. Nawaz for his part had been repeatedly humiliated by the military under Musharraf and eventually came to accept that Benazir represented the least of his headaches. Their reconciliation was formally underlined and confirmed in the Charter of Democracy that the two ex-prime ministers signed at the nearby London home of Benazir's security chief, Rehman Malik.

The signature of the Charter, which committed both sides to fighting against dictatorship and jointly struggling for the restoration of democracy, was attended by high-level party functionaries from both sides. Benazir immediately stopped all criticism of Nawaz, and he in turn from then on referred to her as his 'sister' and partner in the endeavour to create a better Pakistan. Most important of all, they agreed to a power-sharing formula in which Benazir and the PPP would have the first shot at forming a government in the event of an indecisive future election. Nawaz's supporters have never denied the substance of this understanding, including an end to back-stabbing and bribing of legislators to cross party political lines, which continued to hold after her death and the 2008 elections.

London had its advantages, but it was in Dubai that Benazir felt most at ease. This sparkling Gulf metropolis had the additional benefit of being a relatively short distance away from Pakistan and, as a major international airport hub, it was easy to fly from there to any and every part of the world. Dubai was where Benazir's children spent their formative years in school and formed important childhood friendships, where Bakhtawar (Itty for short) and Aseefa developed their taste for Rap music and R'n B that their father dislikes, and where the prestigious Shaikh Rashid School helped Bilawal get the A Levels he needed as a prerequisite for admission to Oxford. Dubai may have lacked the intellectual stimulation of London, but it was comfortable and secure. Friends arriving from abroad would find themselves breakfasting with Benazir in the villa, then being taken off for a mid-morning browse through the aisles of a local supermarket, before ending up at one of Benazir's favourite local restaurants, often a small Italian bistro where the staff were familiar with their VIP visitor's passion for pizza and chocolate fondue.

It was from the comparative safety of her Dubai exile headquarters that Benazir anxiously monitored the disastrous 1999 Kargil war between India and Pakistan. 'Kargil had been Pakistan's beggest blunder,' she would later write:

> The country had lost its eastern wing in 1971 in the face of Indian aggression. That defeat could be passed on to the Indians. But the regime in Pakistan alone was responsible for the Kargil blunder.
>
> In the snow-clad mountains, Pakistani-backed men took up positions they had no hope to keep. Pakistan was made to retreat from the mountain tops in disgrace when it found itself internationally isolated and blamed for the conflict. Instead of announcing the withdrawal from Islamabad in an attempt to keep the country's dignity, the prime minister trotted off to see the US President and 'take dictation' from Washington.

It was from Dubai that Benazir watched helplessly as Musharraf stage-managed the 2002 national referendum to extend his mandate as president for another five years. It was again from Dubai that Benazir followed the results of the October 2002 general elections in which her party garnered the largest number of votes (7.39 million), but gained only 63 seats in the National Assembly. When Zardari was released from prison in 2004, it was to Dubai that he first headed before going on to the United States for medical treatment.

Preparations to leave Pakistan did not get under way until 1998, but Benazir had begun running out of options by early 1996 as the economy began to slide and the PPP was charged with failing to provide effective governance to deal with rising ethnic violence, organized crime, and accusations of serious corruption levelled against Zardari. Relations deteroriated between Benazir and her handpicked president, Farooq Leghari, after Murtaza was killed in a police shoot-out in September 1996. Two months after Benazir hinted that Leghari could have been involved in her brother's death, he took action. Angered by the whisper-campaign started against him, the concerned president sought the backing of army chief Karamat to move against her. Against the backdrop of opposition-sponsored rallies protesting the incompetence of PPP rule, Leghari dismissed her from office on 5 November 1996, established a caretaker government, and ordered fresh elections that paved the way for the return to power of Nawaz Sharif.

Benazir recognized that exile for her would be a form of political death. However, faced with a hostile president, the re-election as prime minister of her unforgiving, arch rival Nawaz, and Zardari's return to prison, she had little choice. The decision over whether to stay home in Pakistan or go abroad came in April 1999 when Benazir was sentenced to five years in jail, banned from politics for five years and, together with Zardari, fined US$8.6 million for alleged corruption during her last term in office.

It was Nusrat's idea to choose Dubai, the principal city of the United Arab Emirates, as the headquarters for her daughter's self-imposed exile and home away from home in Pakistan. When Zulfikar was alive, the Bhuttos had repeatedly hosted visits to Pakistan by Sheikh Zayed bin Sultan Al Nahyan, the ruler of Abu Dhabi and president of the UAE, whose traditional lifestyle included riding and hunting with falcons. Zayed spent weeks on end in the Rahim Yar Khan district of Pakistan hunting for wild deer and bustard. The desert wastes of Pakistan have always been a favoured hunting destination for royal parties from the Gulf, but Zayed was the only Gulf royal gifted with a hunting lodge and private airstrip on the orders of the prime minister, who personally told him how he would always have the run of the place. During his regular visits, the local civil service and police were placed at his disposal, local laws did not apply to his party, and he would fly in direct from Abu Dhabi or Dubai without having to go through Pakistani customs or immigration.

When Zulfikar was on death row, Zayed was among the foreign dignitaries who tried and failed to save his life. After Zulfikar's death, he told Nusrat and the children that they should consider themselves as part of his extended family. This was when Nusrat's health began to progressively deteriorate as Alzheimer's disease took control. Benazir gave her a separate set of rooms on the first floor of the villa where she was looked after by full-time personal staff. After Murtaza's death the two women had kissed and made up, with Benazir telling friends she was determined to do whatever possible to ensure that her mother lived out her final years in dignity.

For as long as they lived, Benazir and her brothers had direct access to Zayed, rent-free accommodation, and money for their expenses. The ruler's only request was that the Bhutto family not allow the politics of Pakistan to be played out among their supporters on the streets of his country. It was a request that Benazir always felt duty bound to honour. She also ensured that whenever she gave an interview to the media from Dubai, there was no reference to where she was based and where she spent so much of her time in exile. These restraints on media contacts did not apply to Benazir's high-level meetings with emissaries of the Pakistan government. In January 2007 she had the first of two critical meetings with Musharraf at a nearby Abu Dhabi hotel. This first meeting was intended to break the ice between the two and boost mutual confidence for later meetings. Follow-up talks were held in June, six months later, by when both sides had worked out the nitty-gritty of what they wanted from each other. Like the January encounter, the US government's footprints were all over the June meeting.

Benazir was businesslike in her approach. She demanded and won Musharraf's agreement to drop all corruption charges against herself and Zardari. This formed the basis of the National Reconciliation Ordinance that was approved the following October and applied as much to Benazir as to any other Pakistani politician, such as Nawaz. Musharraf also agreed to order the freeing of Bhutto family accounts frozen in foreign banks. Benazir's concession was to agree to serve as a future prime minister under Musharraf as a civilian president. To this end, she ordered PPP legislators not to vote against Musharraf later that year when he put himself forward for another five year presidential term. When Musharraf's re-election was voted upon in parliament in October 2007, PPP legislators abstained but did not boycott the process, thus giving Musharraf the legitimacy he required for another term in office.

There was a brief struggle over whether Musharraf should remain as army chief until the election. Benazir argued he should shed his uniform and offer himself as a civilian candidate. In the end it was agreed he would resign as army chief, but only after he had been formally re-elected as president. Those who were present at the June meeting say Musharraf got very emotional, even weepy at one point, when protesting he had nothing personal against Benazir and only had Pakistan's best interests at heart. His PPP critics say he successfully managed to mask his true feelings, and what they describe as his 'generational' hatred for the Bhutto family. This, they say, goes back to the early 1970s when Musharraf's father, Syed Musharrafuddin, was employed as an accountant at the Pakistan embassy in Jakarta from where he was sacked on Zulfikar's direct orders. The charge against him was his alleged role in a scam to import Mercedes cars under diplomatic licence and then sell them for a massive profit in the open market. The younger Musharraf, it was said, promised to avenge his father by pursuing a lifelong vendetta against the Bhutto family.

For her part, Benazir was remarkably composed throughout the June 2007 meeting with Musharraf. If she knew or recalled what had happened to Musharraf's father all those many years ago, and Zulfikar's role in his dismissal and disgrace, she did not refer to it. Exile had at least taught her how to keep her true feelings under control.

EPILOGUE

A DEEPLY DISLIKED MILITARY REGIME HEADED BY GENERAL MUSHARRAF WAS IN CHARGE OF PAKISTAN WHEN Benazir headed home from exile in October 2007. Only 18 months earlier such a move would have been unthinkable, but much had changed in the intervening period to hold out the very real prospect of Benazir being elected as prime minister for a record third term. The new developments effectively neutralized both the PPP government's record of under-achievement and the question marks hanging over Zardari's financial and commercial deals.

The factors that could make such a difference to Benazir's political survival were connected to the ever-increasing unpopularity of Pervez Musharraf. Like the military rulers before him, Musharraf had promised early elections after his 1999 coup toppled the democratically elected government of Pakistan. Just as those previous military rulers, he reneged on his promise. 'Musharraf and his generals are determined to stay on in power,' commented Pakistani academic Professor Pervez Hoodbhoy.

> They will protect the source of their power—the army. They will accommodate those they must—the Americans. They will pander to the

mullahs. They will crush those who threaten their power and privilege, and ignore the rest. No price is too high for them. They are the reason why Pakistan fails.

Among the reasons for the steep decline in support for Musharraf were the human rights violations that were carried out by the security forces in the name of making Pakistan safe from Islamic extremists. The crackdown on such extremists was always selective because Musharraf also needed the jihadi community as an insurance card to remind the Americans of his own indispensable role in battling the forces of Islamic terror. The problems with this strategy was that it gave Pakistan's secret services free licence to arrest, imprison, and torture at will. As individual 'suspects' were plucked off the streets by one of the country's many security agencies, comparisons were drawn with the scandal of the forced disappearances that had been a feature of the worst Latin American dictatorships two decades earlier.

When Chief Justice Iftikhar Muhammad Chaudhry began probing the scandal of missing persons in 2006, he and other fellow supreme court judges were arrested and dismissed from their jobs. The fallout from the arrests of the judges was immediate and severe. By the middle of 2007, according to a survey carried out by a US-based institution, the International Republican Institute, Musharraf's approval ratings at home in Pakistan had dropped from 63 per cent to an all time low of 26 per cent. For a US administration that relished the support and backing he offered whenever there was a strike against Islamic militant bases along the Pakistan–Afghan border, the rising unpopularity of its 'indispensable ally' was nothing short of an unmitigated disaster.

To shore him up and ensure he remained on top as an American asset, a team of experts from the White House, National Security Council, and State Department crafted a brand new political alliance between Musharraf and Benazir, Pakistan's most popular grassroots politician. Never mind that laws passed at Musharraf's direction blocked Benazir from ever again holding public office, or that Benazir herself had grave misgivings about working together with Musharraf.

There were higher considerations involved affecting US interests in the region. 'They [the White House] finally came to understand that Benazir was the only way to save Musharraf,' recalls her American lobbyist Mark Siegel. 'They didn't have an epiphany one day and realize that she was the daughter of democracy or whatever. They just saw her and used her.'

Under US prodding, Musharraf flew to Abu Dhabi in January 2007 to hold the first of his confidential, face-to-face meetings with Benazir. At that first meeting he agreed to change the law that prevented twice-elected prime ministers from ever serving again. Musharraf's US-backed tactics to win over Benazir were matched in Washington by carefully calibrated plans to bring the former prime minister back into the fold. Suddenly, the Benazir who had been effectively boycotted by the Bush administration found herself being courted by the same senior US officials who had previously not even had the courtesy to acknowledge her telephone calls.

Siegel, who remembers how she was cold-shouldered, said:

My wife and I would have events for her at our home, we would invite all the appropriate people from the Administration. If anyone came at all, it would be the Pakistan desk officer at the State Department.

At events where we had senators from the Foreign Relations Committee, people at the highest level, the Administration would cold shoulder and ignore her because it didn't want to offend Musharraf.

The process of rehabilitating Benazir began with contacts established with Assistant Secretary of State Richard Boucher, and this was followed up by his senior colleague, Under Secretary of State Nicholas Burns. Telephone calls—at least two in mid-2007 according to Siegel—were made to Benazir by Secretary of State Condoleezza Rice and the diplomatic wooing was wrapped up in the late summer of 2007 by the US ambassador to the UN, Zalmay Khalilzad, a trusted member of Bush's inner circle. In August 2007 Khalilzad and Benazir had a series of meetings in New York before flying out together to Aspen, Colorado, in a private plane to participate in a luncheon for prominent US business and political leaders.

Just prior to the talks with Khalilzad, Benazir had her last face-to-face meeting in Abu Dhabi with Musharraf, where he outlined his National Reconciliation Ordinance to withdraw all cases of corruption against leading politicians. The quid pro quo was Benazir promising to support his staying on as a civilian president after parliamentary elections scheduled for early 2008. Whether Musharraf ever intended to follow through and keep his side of the bargain by permitting Benazir to participate in elections and assume office again if elected remains a moot point. One school of thought believes he was prepared to please the Americans by withdrawing all corruption cases against her and Zardari, and going through the motions of appearing to work with her. The anecdotal evidence, however, suggests there remained a deep reluctance to take the next step of actually sharing power with Benazir. As former Zulfikar media adviser Khalid Hassan observed, 'The generals never liked the Bhuttos because the Bhuttos always asserted authority— and they didn't like it.'

British newspaper reporter Christina Lamb has never forgotten the conversation she had with Musharraf after he seized power in 1999, when he said of Benazir, 'More than anyone else she had the brains and opportunity to change Pakistan and she didn't do it, instead spending her time making money. As long as I am here, she will never be allowed back in power.' Siegel remembers Musharraf as charming, respectful, and even deferential to Benazir. 'But at the end of the day he would never follow through ... she understood that for whatever reason even if he wanted to, he wasn't able to follow through.' The Bush administration believed otherwise. Senior US officials were convinced they had a dream team in the making if Musharraf and Benazir agreed to work in tandem.

When Benazir said goodbye to her children in Dubai before leaving for Karachi on 18 October 2007, she had the blessings and approval of everyone who mattered in Washington DC. She flew back home to a country simmering with violence; a country where there had been five attempts in as many years to assassinate the president. A few months prior to her return, in July 2007, militants fired on Musharraf's aircraft as it took off from a military base in Rawalpindi. Police later recovered a long-barrelled anti-aircraft gun and a machine-gun from a nearby rooftop. In 2006, Pakistan's Supreme Court upheld death sentences against 12 men convicted of taking part in two attempts to kill the president. One of the convicted men, Islam Siddiqui, had been hanged earlier in 2005. In 2004, Abu Faraj Farj al Liby, described by Pakistani security forces as the Al Qa'eda number 3, and Amjad Farooqi were gunned down after being accused of participating in anti-Musharraf plots. In 2003, a Pakistani court handed down 10-year sentences to each of three militants accused of participating in an assassination plot against Musharraf. The president also narrowly escaped two attempts on his life in December 2003 alone. The first was when a bomb blew up under a bridge just minutes before his convoy drove over. The second, on Christmas day, was when two suicide trucks were driven into his convoy travelling on the same road in Rawalpindi.

In her posthumously published book, *Reconciliation: Islam, Democracy and the West* (2008), Benazir writes of the enormous crowds 'that exceeded my wildest dreams and expectations' turning out to greet her in Karachi. 'It was truly breathtaking,' she writes, with music pulsating from boom boxes, supporters dancing around the cavalcade and others hanging from trees and telephone poles to catch a glimpse of Benazir and other PPP leaders as they made their way to the city centre.

Benazir had been warned she could be the victim of an assassination attempt, but she was sitting back unprepared and exhausted in her armour-plated truck when sniper fire was heard just after midnight, and a bomb was detonated nearby. Among those travelling with Benazir that night was former Pakistan ambassador to the US, Syeda Abida Hussain, who believes the bomb was an improvised explosive device (IED) tied to a baby's leg. 'There was somebody in the crowd who was trying to hand this baby to her,' recalls Abida.

> And BB was so moved that she put her arms forward as if to take the baby. But the crowd was at a distance, it was not next to her and she was up on the truck.
>
> When she saw the baby, she then made gestures to stop, then she sent her

security people. The security people went and the baby was thrown into a vehicle and obviously that was the vehicle next to the truck that exploded. Obviously the baby died as well. I was splattered with human flesh and blood, I had bits of flesh in my hair—it was just an awful thing to live through.

At least 130 people were killed and hundreds of others wounded in the shocking outrage, prompting Benazir to write a confidential letter to Musharraf in which she named the Pakistani officials allegedly plotting to kill her. Citing information she said had come from contacts in neighbouring Afghanistan, Benazir told journalists she understood that four suicide squads had been despatched to kill her. These squads were allegedly working in tandem with the officials Benazir named, including two retired high-ranking Pakistan intelligence operatives, alleged to be retired Intelligence Bureau chief and ex-Brigadier Ejaz Hussain Shah and former ISI chief Hamid Gul.

It was a measure of her distrust of Musharraf that she also sent a private message to Siegel saying that Musharraf would bear some of the blame if she were to be assassinated. 'Nothing will, God willing, happen,' she said in her abbreviated email message.

> Just wanted you to know if it does, in addition to the names in my letter to Musharraf of October 16th, I would hold Musharraf responsible. I have been made to feel insecure by his minions and there is no way what is happening in terms of stopping me from taking private cars or using tinted windows or giving jammers or four police mobiles to cover all sides could happen without him.

Siegel never saw the letter that was sent to Musharraf through diplomatic channels, but, as he elaborated,

> What was interesting about the October 16 letter that she sent to Musharraf is that it was based on inside intelligence reports from a Gulf nation and they were just trying to be helpful and friendly. But Musharraf did nothing to investigate any of those people.

> At least the PPP and others I speak to every day think there was direct involvement. I don't know that we think Musharraf ordered it, I'm sure he didn't. But you know it's like Thomas Beckett, "Will no one rid me of this

troublesome priest?" So I think that whoever did it thought Musharraf would not be displeased.

In retrospect, what happened in Karachi now seems almost like a dress-rehearsal—although its deadly intent was never in doubt—for the attack two months later that killed Benazir as she was addressing a pre-election rally in Rawalpindi. As she left the Rawalpindi rally in a white, armour-plated Land Cruiser in the early evening of 27 December, a gunman detonated a bomb after shooting her in the neck and head. PPP political adviser Safdar Abbasi told the media later that Benazir had been 'smiling and happy' as she walked away from the podium from which she had addressed the rally. 'She took me inside the car and sat in front of me. I started chanting slogans because there were crowds all around.' Abbasi, his wife Naheed, PPP Vice President Maqdoom Amin Fahim, and Laiq, a member of Benazir's personal staff, were all bundled in with her as the car began to move. 'All of a sudden there was the sound of firing. I heard the sound of a bullet. I saw her [Benazir]: she looked as though she ducked in when she heard the firing,' Abbasi said. 'We did not realize that she had been hit by a bullet.' Only minutes earlier, as she addressed the crowd, Benazir turned to Abbasi and invited him to stand next to her: 'Why don't you join me?' she asked him.

It was Abbasi's wife, Naheed, who tended to the dying Benazir, ripping off her own headscarf to try and staunch the blood that was flowing down her neck and across her long blue shirt. 'She was so happy, so thrilled that the rally had gone so well that she got into the car, turned to me and kissed me on my left cheek, then on my right cheek,' Khan told the media later. She heard Benazir say, 'There are so many people waving, please open the sunroof so I can wave back.'

> The next thing, I heard what I thought was a firecracker. I had no idea she had been shot. She fell back into the car and I thought as she sat down and slumped on to me without saying a single word that she was exhausted ... then I felt something warm dripping on to me, which is when I started screaming. I realized it was her blood and that the silence meant she had died, perhaps instantly, and I hope painlessly ... We raced to Rawalpindi General Hospital but I knew it was too late. We had lost her.

Detonations set off immediately afterwards peppered the Land Cruiser with shrapnel.

Hours after she was buried the following day next to her father in Larkana, Pakistan's Interior Ministry claimed that the case had been solved, placing the responsibility for the killing on Pakistan Taliban leader Baitullah Masud who is based in the tribal areas of north-west Pakistan. Officials claimed they had recorded a telephone conversation in which he had accepted responsibility. The claim was immediately denied by Masud's spokesman who described the recorded telephone conversation as a fabrication. He told the French news agency AFP, 'This is a conspiracy of the government, army and intelligence agencies', adding that it was against tribal tradition to attack women.

There was also speculation that the US was somehow involved because, so the story went, the Americans had always distrusted the Bhuttos. Some recalled how the US authorities appeared to be reluctant until the end to plead for clemency when Zia refused to commute Zulfikar's death sentence in 1979. Disregarding the many friends and supporters Benazir had in the US, starting with Peter Galbraith and including many senators and congressmen, others recalled a line in Benazir's autobiography, *Daughter of the East*, following the death in Cannes of her younger brother, Shahnawaz, who had been planning to return to Afghanistan when he was found dead. Benazir wrote: 'Had Zia got hold of Shah's plan and pre-empted it? Or had the CIA killed him as a friendly gesture towards their favourite dictator.' Reacting to reports of a possible Washington connection to Benazir's death, a spokeswoman for the US embassy in Islamabad said, 'The suggestion of US involvement is completely outrageous and unfounded.'

There were a handful of even more outrageous claims that Pakistan's traditional enemy across the border, India, was also somehow involved. In actuality, India has consistently been in favour of democratically elected leaders in Pakistan because they are deemed to be less likely to encourage war with India, and there was what amounted to a history of friendly family contacts that stretched back decades. Indira Gandhi was among the first foreign leaders to plead for clemency for Zulfikar and, when he was hanged, she willingly hosted a visit to Delhi by both Murtaza and Shahnawaz. Benazir was in a category of her own. When she first set foot in India during the S[h]imla summit one local newspaper rhapsodied, 'Benazir is Benazir', punning on the meaning of her name (beyond comparison). Many thoughtful Indians also acknowledged the role she had played in reducing bilateral tensions and the 'good atmosphere' created after her meeting with Rajiv Gandhi soon after her 1988 election.

After her assassination, Indian Prime Minister Dr Manmohan Singh said in a generous tribute:

> In her death the subcontinent has lost an outstanding leader who worked for democracy and reconciliation in her country.
>
> The manner of her going is a reminder of the common dangers that our region faces from cowardly acts of terrorism and of the need to eradicate this dangerous threat.

When it came to India, she was brutally honest, yet was free from any sense of personal vindictiveness towards her powerful neighbour across the border. The manner in which Benazir was assassinated remains all-important in determining who was ultimately responsible. If, as is widely believed, she died after being shot in the neck at point blank range, the finger of responsibility points to someone within the ruling Pakistani establishment responsible for the essential personal security that should have blocked a gunman from getting close. It was so much more convenient for the government to claim that it was the bomb blast and the subsequent skull fracture she sustained that was responsible for her death. Conveniently, this is the style of killing, rather than sniper shots, favoured by the Taliban.

To begin with, the Interior Ministry agreed that Benazir had died from bullet wounds. Hours later Interior Minister Hamid Nawaz Khan said the government still stood by the 'factual position' that she died from a skull fracture and not from a bullet. The Interior Ministry would later cite in support of its findings a report issued by Scotland Yard investigators who said there was sufficient evidence to suggest that

Benazir died of severe head injuries 'sustained as a consequence of the bomb blast and due to head impact somewhere in the escape hatch of the vehicle'. Despite the Scotland Yard report, the conspiracy theories refused to die down. PPP activists would later claim that Benazir had been successfully targeted by laser beam technology. As this is the kind of technology that is only available to US forces serving in Iraq, so the theory went, it could have been accessed only by the government of Pakistan, presumably for use against the Taliban, who handed it over to Benazir's killers. In support of this particular theory, the doctor who treated Benazir upon arrival at Rawalpindi General Hospital, Dr M. Musaddiq Khan, was also cited as saying that the wounds she suffered were not from bullets and that some of her brain and blood had spilt over from her head.

Addressing the security issue, Pakistan's ambassador to the US, Mahmud Ali Durrani, said:

> She was surrounded by police vehicles. And had it not been one of the police vehicles which took the blast in Karachi, unfortunately she would have died there.
>
> There was a bubble of security. The PPP insisted that they have their own private loyalists around. They were there too. And there were about 7,800 to 8,000 security people deployed just for that. That is more security than anybody deploys anywhere in the world.
>
> I think the government of Pakistan provided her all the security that was necessary ... so it's just a blame-game.

A simple exhumation would have resolved the blame-game issue once and for all, but Asif Zardari declared he wanted his wife to be left in peace and rejected the autopsy request because he did not trust the government. Both Benazir and her supporters had pleaded for weeks before with the authorities in Islamabad to improve the security around her, apparently to no avail. Sherry Rehman, a close friend and confidante of Benazir, related how 'We had been in constant correspondence with the Interior Ministry to provide her better protection, but had gotten no joy or relief from them other than the provision of a few pointless leader police patrols.' Rehman, who was entrusted with washing her dead friend's body, said in a widely quoted comment:

> What I saw on her neck at the back of her head on the left side was a huge gaping bullet wound that went in on the left side, came out the other. And it is recorded on private channels in Pakistan that everybody saw a trained assassin cock his gun at her, take aim, and deliver the fatal bullet wound that made her slump down immediately into the car and she bled profusely for hours and died. We feel she even died before she reached the hospital.

In her now famous comment to me a few years before she died, Benazir said elections had repeatedly proven that she was the most popular leader in Pakistan.

> Therefore for a series of people I must be eliminated. The first successor [Zia] tried to eliminate me, to impose a one party rule in the country. Now the military wants to eliminate me because they want the MMA [Mutahida Majlis-e-Amal alliance of religious parties] to be the only alternative in the country.

Benazir's tragic death is a victory for Pakistan's military establishment and the Islamic fundamentalists who despised her. On the other hand, even some of her most ardent supporters would agree that the legacy she leaves is not without its blemishes. The contradictions in her personality that were so evident at the start of her political career remained with her throughout her life. A feudal princess and a democrat at the same time, an ardent women's rights campaigner and yet a status quo prime minister where women were concerned, a peace campaigner and a clandestine promoter of Pakistan's missile and nuclear capabilities. For all the contradictions, I like to think that Benazir did evolve over the years. Certainly, the spoilt young university student who threw ashtrays at the servants in Larkana was not the same as the young woman who endured the agony of her father's death and her own stints of imprisonment before she became a significant political player in her own right.

In turn, the 35-year-old prime minister was very different from the older and wiser 50-year-old eking out her exile in Dubai and London. Benazir's abiding tragedy was her failure to control Pakistan's military and intelligence services. Right to the end of her life she was convinced that a combination of the army and secret service agencies was out to destroy her. History may yet prove her right. Recent research carried out in Pakistan has disclosed how the army uses a civilian front to control everything from petrol pumps to banks, insurance companies and universities. There is little or no accountability for the generals who use five welfare foundations to operate a private business empire worth an estimated US$10 billion, which is run as a state within a state.

Some of Benazir's gravest errors, such as supporting the Taliban from their embryonic original state, personally participating in Pakistan's nuclear exports to North Korea, and the needlessly provocative statements firing up the jihadis in Kashmir can be seen in the context of her trying to cosy up to Pakistan's ruthless generals and spy chiefs. The ultimate irony is that the Taliban she helped to create have been blamed for her murder.

Regrettably for Benazir, she failed to develop the skills needed to deal with these parallel centres of power. 'To some extent you could argue there is a Bhutto family curse,' commented Teresita Schaffer, director of South Asia programmes at the Center for Strategic International Studies in Washington DC. 'In most cases it has been a historical rift between her family and the military. That has ensured that she has always struggled to rule when she has been in power.' Following Benazir's death the generals agreed to retreat to their barracks, but they have the means and the incentive to assert themselves in the future if civilian political parties fail to arrive at a long-term understanding about how to share power. During his lifetime Murtaza used to argue that the only way to control the army in the long term was to arm every Pakistani citizen with a kalashnikov and a box of hand-grenades. Benazir's solution was democracy, but it remains to be seen what lasting contribution she made to the building of viable democratic institutions as an alternative to military rule.

Towards the end of her life Benazir increasingly saw success for herself and Pakistan through the prism of family life, but family life only in the strictly narrow sense of her own husband and children. The idea of family did not extend to Murtaza who was kept at a deliberate distance from both party and government, prompting one critic to comment, 'The last of the great Mughals, Aurangzeb, is very unpopular because he imprisoned his father and killed his brothers for the sake of power. People compare her to Aurangzeb because she is trying to do to her only brother what the Emperor did to his family.'

When Zulfikar was alive, his daughter's devotion to him was exemplary. After he died, Benazir's bonds of loyalty were in time transferred to her husband. The perfect daughter became the ideal wife. Like Zulfikar, Zardari could do no wrong. She also developed a sense of dynasty, absent in her as a younger woman, invoking the inevitable comparisons with other prominent South Asian political families, such as the Nehru–Gandhis in India, the Bandaranaikes in Sri Lanka, and Sheikh Mujibur Rahman's descendants in Bangladesh. Five years before she was assassinated Benazir was asked what aspirations she had for her children. At that time she spoke of a lawyer's role for Bilawal and of how she hoped her daughters might consider future careers as social workers. Yet, only months before her death, what emerged was her hope that Bilawal would one day become the ruler of Pakistan in his own right. If he does indeed succeed, he will be the fourth successive Bhutto after Sir Shahnawaz, Zulfikar, and Benazir to take on the duties and responsibilities of political office.

On the other hand, Benazir's controversial decision to anoint Bilawal as her political heir could prove to be a poisoned chalice for her immediate family, the wider Bhutto clan, and the rest of Pakistan. Some day in the future Bilawal may have to fight Murtaza's son and his first cousin, Zulfikar junior, to claim his dynastic legacy. Zulfikar junior has a half sister in fiery Fatima, just as Bilawal has two sisters, Bakhtawar and Aseefa. Bilawal's other dead uncle, Shahnawaz, also left a daughter, Sassi, although she and her mother, Rehana, have not been seen in recent years in Pakistan. The script-writers of Pakistan's emerging film industry, affectionately referred to as Lollywood, must surely see the potential of this several part family drama that could rage unresolved for the coming 100 years.

Khuda hafiz (God be with you), Benazir; Shahzadi, goodbye.

INDEX

Abbasi, Naheed, 120
Abbasi, Safdar, 108, 120
Afghanistan, X, 12, 43, 44, 49, 52, 64, 90, 94, 100, 119, 121
Ahsan, Aitzaz, 108-09
Al Zulfikar, 20, 23, 47
Ali, Mazhar, 21
Ali, Tariq, 21, 26-27
Anwar, Raja, 60
Arabs, XIII, 101-02
Army, Pakistan, 7, 17, 20, 22, 43, 57, 59, 73, 76, 77, 81, 82, 83, 84, 85, 87, 93, 94, 95, 96, 99, 100, 102, 103, 114, 121, 124-25
Awami League, 81
Ayala, Luis, 108

Babar, Major General Nasirullah, 61, 100
Baluchistan, 17, 73, 91
Bandaranaike, Srimavo, 22, 126
Bangladesh, XII, 3, 7, 60, 62, 64, 65, 80, 126
Barak, Daphne, 5
BBC, 6, 30, 72
Beg, General Aslam, 84, 85, 89, 91, 93, 94, 95, 97
Beg, Mohammed, 103
Bhutto, Fatima, 26-27, 32, 103, 126
Bhutto, Ghinwa, 24
Bhutto, Khursheed Begum, 13, 83

Bhutto, Mir Ghulam Murtaza, 12
Bhutto, Mir Murtaza, XIII, XIV, 7, 8, 14, 18, 19, 20, 23-27, 28, 31, 38, 47, 56, 59-60, 83, 102, 103, 105, 106, 107, 111, 122, 125
Bhutto, Nusrat, XIV, 9, 11, 12, 14, 17, 18, 19, 20, 25, 26, 29, 30, 32, 33, 38, 47, 48, 49, 53, 91, 102, 107, 111, 112
Bhutto, Sanam, 13, 14, 20, 48, 56, 60, 107
Bhutto, Shireen Amir Begum, 11
Bhutto, Sir Shahnawaz, 12-13, 59, 83, 126
Bhutto, Zulfikar Ali, X, XII, 7, 12, 19, 22, 46, 48, 49, 50, 82, 84, 102, 111
Bombay, 11, 12, 13
Boucher, Richard, 116
Buckley, James, 48
Bukhari, Murtaza, 31
Burns, John, 32-33
Burns, Nicholas, 116
Bush administration, 56, 116, 117
Bush, George H. W., 55, 116

Carver, Jeremy, 31-32
Charter of Democracy, 109
Chaudhry, Chief Justice Iftikhar, 86-87, 115
China, 40, 69, 75
CIA, 45, 51, 70-71, 100, 121

Clinton administration, 71
Clinton, Bill, 47
Combined Opposition Parliamentary Front, 97
Combined Opposition Parliamentary Party, 97
Commonwealth, 98
Confidence-building measures, 61
Corruption, 26, 29-32, 86, 87, 99, 111, 112-13, 117

Dar, Ishaq, 108
Daughter of the East, 13, 14, 28, 121
Democracy, 10, 18, 23, 47, 67, 82, 84, 87, 94, 96, 99, 109, 116, 118, 122, 125
Devaud, Daniel, 31-32, 37, 86
Dubai, XII, 4, 9, 31, 33, 35, 38, 42, 63, 67, 104, 105, 109-10, 111, 112, 117, 124
Durrani, Mahmud Ali, 123

East Pakistan, 8, 16, 80-81
Einstein, Albert, 70
Election, General, XI, XIII, 53, 86, 110
Fahim, Makdoom Amin, 86, 120
Farooqi, Amjad, 118
Feisal, King, 16
France, 36, 69, 74

Galbraith, John Kenneth, XII, 8, 45, 46
Galbraith, Peter, XII, 8, 45-57, 121
Gandhi, Indira, 3, 6, 16, 22, 59-60, 121-22, 128
Gandhi, Rajiv, 57, 60-61, 62, 98, 122, 128
Gandhi, Sonia, 61
Gautier, François, 62
Gopal, Neena, 4
Gul, General Hamid, 81, 85, 89, 91, 94-95, 97, 98, 118

Haq, Dr Mahbub ul, 93
Haq, General Zia ul, 4, 9, 37, 74, 81, 82, 90
Harvard, XII, 1, 6, 7, 8, 14-15, 16, 46, 47, 52, 53, 60, 73, 104, 105, 106, 107

Hasan, Khalid, XII, 75
Hasan, Wajid Shamsul, 86, 91, 95, 98
Hijacking, 23-24, 47, 92
Hinton, Deanne, 45, 50-52
Howard, Sir Michael, 8
Human rights, 2, 17, 48, 101, 115
Hussain, Ejaz, 119
Hussain, Syeda Abida, 118

IMF, 56
India, XII, XIII, 3, 5, 6, 7, 8, 9, 12, 13, 14, 16, 30, 32, 39, 40, 41, 45-46, 52, 57, 58-66, 69, 72, 73, 76, 80, 83, 84, 85, 93, 95, 98, 99, 110, 121, 122, 126
Iqbal, Ahsan, 108
Iran, 11, 37, 41, 67, 70-71, 78, 79, 101
ISI, 77-78, 79, 81-82, 85, 89-90, 91, 94, 95, 100, 119
Islamabad, 9, 32, 40, 41, 42, 45, 48, 49, 51, 58, 60-61, 67, 68, 96, 97, 102, 110, 121, 123
Isphahani, Mirza Muhammad Abdul Latif, 12
Israel, XIII, 5
Jafri, Wasim, 93
Jagmohan, 61
Jails, 18, 47
Jalalabad, 94-95
Jatoi, Ghulam Mustafa, 97, 99
Jeddah, 108
Jehangir, Asma, 2
Jews, XIII, 55
Jinnah, Quaid-e-Azam, 13
Junagadh, 13

Kakar, Wahid, 82
Kalam, Abdul, 40
Kallu, General Shamsur Rahman, 81
Karachi, X, 12, 13, 14, 15, 17, 22, 25, 26, 33, 47, 48, 51, 52, 54, 65, 68-69, 76, 95, 99, 105, 117, 118, 120, 123
Karamat, Jehangir, 82, 111
Kargil, 85, 95, 110
Kashmir, 60, 61-62, 63, 85, 90, 93, 95, 98, 100, 125
Keating, Paul, 35

Kennedy, Jacqueline, 45
Kennedy, John F., 15
Khalilzad, Zalmay, 116-17
Khan, A.Q., 40-41, 43, 67-73, 76, 77, 78
Khan, Dr M. Musaddiq, 123
Khan, General Ayub, 17, 82, 98
Khan, General Tikka, 80-81, 94
Khan, General Yahya, 81, 82
Khan, Ghulam Ishaq, 53, 55, 74, 76, 82, 89, 93, 94, 96, 97, 98, 99
Khan, Hamid Nawaz, 122-23
Khan, Imran, XII, 34
Khan, Jemima, 34
Khan, Munir Ahmed, 71, 73, 74, 75, 76
Khan, Sahibzada Yakub, 48-49, 93
Kissinger, Henry, 15
Korea, North, 9, 40-43, 64, 67-68, 71, 78, 90, 99, 125

Lahore, 10, 16, 17, 18, 20, 21, 22, 32, 46, 54, 64, 96, 108, 109
Lai, Chou En, 15
Landlord, feudal, X, 12
Larkana, X, XIII, XIV, 3, 12, 21, 25, 53, 54, 121, 124
Leghari, Farooq, 82, 99, 111
Liby, Abu Faraj Farj al, 118
Libya, 5, 16, 41, 67, 70, 71, 78, 79, 101-02
London, XI, XII, 4, 5, 6, 9, 12, 20, 21, 25, 27, 29, 30, 31, 33, 35, 36, 42, 52, 63, 68, 70, 72, 86, 91, 98, 107, 108, 109, 110, 124

Mahmood, Sultan Bashiruddin, 73
Malik, Rehman, 109
Masud, Baitullah, 121
Masud, Jehangir, 20
Military, Pakistan, XII, I, 9, 10, 14, 17, 18, 20, 21, 24, 33, 34, 39, 41, 42, 48, 49, 56, 58, 64, 67, 76, 77, 78, 79, 80, 81, 83, 85, 88, 89, 90, 92, 93, 94, 98, 99, 108, 109, 114, 118, 124, 125
Mirza, Maj Gen Iskander, 82
Missile programme, 6, 9, 39-43, 67, 68, 99, 124

Mohammed, Prophet, 2, 61
Movement for the Restoration of Democracy (MRD), 18, 47, 84, 94
MQM party, 99
Mujahiddin, 45, 61, 85, 94
Musharraf, Pervez, 34, 36, 55, 56, 67, 78, 79, 81, 82, 84, 85, 86, 87, 88, 95, 108, 109, 110, 112, 113, 114, 115, 116, 117, 118, 119, 120
Musharrafuddin, Syed, 113
Muslim League, 13, 108
Mutahida Majlis-e-Amal (MMA), 10, 124

Nahyan, Shelkh Zayed bin Suktan Al, 111
National Assembly, 29, 35, 53, 82, 110
National People Party, 97
National Reconciliation Ordinance, 113, 117
Nawaz, Asif, 82
Necklace episode, 36-37, 38
Nehru, Jawaharlal, 59, 126
Nehru, Motilal, 59
No-confidence motion, 82, 97
Nodong, 42, 43
North-West Frontier Province (NWFP), 91
Nuclear programme, XIII, 6, 9, 39, 40, 41, 42, 45, 49, 61, 63-64, 67-79, 80, 85, 90, 93, 101, 124, 125

Oakley, Robert, 45, 55, 77, 92
Oxford, X, XI, XII, XIII, I, 2, 3, 4, 6, 7, 8, 9, 12, 15, 16, 17, 19, 20, 23, 29, 34, 39, 46, 47, 52, 53, 63, 73, 104, 105, 106, 107, 110

Pakistan Muslim League (PML-N), 108
Pakistan Peoples Party (PPP), 13, 18, 19, 20, 21, 22, 24, 25, 26, 29, 37, 38, 43, 47, 53, 54, 55, 63, 81, 82, 84, 85, 86, 87, 90, 91, 92, 94, 97, 99, 100, 101, 102, 107, 108, 109, 111, 113, 114, 118, 119, 120, 123
Partition, 12, 59, 64

Pell, Senator Claiborne, 47, 48-49, 50, 52
Percy, Senator Charles, 48-49, 52
Punjab, 22, 61, 62, 81, 91, 96-97
Pyongyang, 9, 41, 42, 67, 68, 90

Qadhafy, Colonel Muammar, 16, 70-71, 101-02
Qasim, Malik, 94

Rabani, Raza, 108
Rahim, Captain Tariq, 24
Rahman, Sheikh Mujibur, 7, 81, 126
Raphel, Arnold, 22
Rawalpindi, 18, 26, 70, 81, 118, 120, 123
Razak, Abdul, 79
Reconciliation: Islam, Democracy and the West, 118
Rehman, General Mujibur, 37
Rehman, Sherry, 123-24
Rice, Condoleezza, 116
Rockwood estate, 32-35, 37
Roper, Hugh Trevor, 7

Sadat, Anwar, 16
Sarwar, Beena, 37
Saudi Arabia, 2, 16, 86, 108
Schaffer, Teresita, 125
Schlegelmilch, Jens, 31-32, 37
Scotland Yard, 122-23
Shah, Abdullah, 26
Shah, Ejaz Hussain, 119
Sharif, Nawaz, 32, 34, 36, 82, 86, 92, 96, 97, 99, 108, 109, 111, 113
Shia Muslims, 12
S[h]imla summit, XIII, XIV, 3, 9, 122
Siddiqui, Islam, 118
Siegel, Mark, 55, 116, 117, 119
Sindh, X, 2, 12, 22, 25, 26, 47, 91, 99, 102, 105
Singh, Dr Manmohan, 122
Singh, V.P., 57

Sirohey, Admiral Iftikhar Ahmed, 94
South Asia, XII, 4, 6, 39, 40, 47, 48, 51, 53, 61, 65, 104, 125, 126
Soviet Union, 42, 45, 64
Sunni Muslims, 12
Supreme Court, 18, 22, 87, 91, 94, 115, 118
Symington amendment, 49

Taliban, 45, 61, 90, 100, 121, 122, 123, 125
Taxes, 33, 34
Thapar, Karan, 4
Thatcher, Margaret, 11
Troika, 89-97, 99

Uddin, Col Rafi, 84
United Arab Emirates, 104, 111
United Nations, 7, 11, 13, 16, 60, 116
US aid, 45, 49, 56, 58
US, Senate Foreign Relations Committee, 47, 48, 50, 51, 56

Waite, Terry, 23
War, Indo-Pak 1965, 13, 60
War, Indo-Pak 1971, XII, 7, 16, 60, 69, 80
War, Indo-Pak Kargil (1999), 85, 110
War, Indo-Pak Proxy, 62, 64
War, Second World, 51, 64
Wolpert, Stanley, 12
Women rights, 2, 4, 19, 96, 100-01, 121, 124

Zardari, Asif Ali, 2, 4, 22, 26-27, 29, 30, 31, 32, 33, 34, 35, 36, 37, 38, 53, 103, 104, 105, 107, 110, 111, 113, 114, 117, 123, 126
Zardari, Bilawal, 22, 30, 90-91, 110, 126
Zardari, Hakim Ali, 29
Zardari, Zarin, 29